Harold G. Koenig, MD
Tracy Lamar, MDiv
Betty Lamar, BFA

A Gospel for the Mature Years: Finding Fulfillment by Knowing and Using Your Gifts

Pre-publication
REVIEWS,
COMMENTARIES,
EVALUATIONS . . .

"**A** *Gospel for the Mature Years* is a book that should be read by all pastors, preferably by all who have elderly people for whom they care, and by anyone at retirement age and above. It assumes that Christian ministry does not cease once one retires and is mindful of the need to let go of some leadership while taking up other active ministry. At the same time, the book is very conscious of the need to work within limits, recognizing that burnout is a spiritual malady that fails to recognize personal limitations. Limitations, however, are no barrier to useful and necessary ministry, and the authors suggest many ideas and a wonderful three-page gifts inventory to help the reader ascertain gifts and recogize abilities.

This is a book packed with ideas, full of intelligent discussion, practical in its advice, and centered upon the work of God in our lives as much as our work for God in the church. It covers all aspects of using gifts in ministry without falling into the trap of mistaking activism for ministry. An excellent book and easy to read, use, and apply."

Terence Kelshaw, DTh, DMin, DD
Right Reverend, Episcopal Bishop,
Diocese of the Rio Grande,
Albuquerque, New Mexico

D1409866

" "**I**s this all there is?' is the disturbing question raised by many older adults when they look through the prism of retirement, trying to recover a sense of value and purpose that, for some, was derived from their former employment. Obviously, the answer is not in function but in vision–of oneself and the surrounding community. *A Gospel for the Mature Years* is a wonderful guide that provides clarity and insight for that vision.

It is a highly readable work that combines excellent source material from both scripture and the medical community, offering solid insights into human behavior and spiritual growth. *A Gospel for the Mature Years* is a combination textbook/workbook that I highly recommend for use in older adult classes and mission groups."

W. Douglas Cole, DMin
Executive Director,
Council on Christian Life
and Public Affairs,
Baptist State Convention
of North Carolina

"**A** *Gospel for the Mature Years: Finding Fulfillment by Knowing and Using Your Gifts* is itself a gift to all who are even beginning to reflect with fear and trepidation about the aging process. Deeply rooted in scriptural reflection, this book is unabashedly Christian in orientation; Christ is the fixed point from which personal assessment and life-planning begins. Because of this, the book is countercultural–it challenges (from God's point of view) our deepest feelings about our own aging, particularly the feeling that we are of less value to humankind when we become frail and are a so-called 'burden' to caregivers. Always conscious of the responsibility of elders to share their gifts with the next generation, *A Gospel* also provides a robust 'wake-up' call to re-think the concept of retirement, by implicitly asking the question throughout, 'Can a Christian ever retire?' The answer, of course, is No! We are *active* followers of Christ until our last breath is taken, even if we are paralyzed and living in a nursing home bed.

Though steeped in both biblical and psychological references, the book is very engaging and easy to read; the questions at the end of each chapter provide excellent material for study groups or Sunday school classes. This is a much-needed challenge to the rapidly aging Christian community, as well as to those who are interested in the way Christianity 'plays out' when confronted with the difficult realities and special joys of the later years."

Jane M. Thibault, PhD
Clinical Gerontologist;
Assistant Professor of Family
and Community Medicine,
University of Louisville
School of Medicine

~~~

"**P**icture a lay person over fifty years of age who comes to the realization that retirement is not far ahead. Add the fact that this person has led a life too busy to allow time for quiet reflection about what it means to believe in God. What would be helpful? Countless theological texts are available, but hardly any speak directly to this prospective reader who hardly knows how to begin a long-delayed pilgrimage of faith and personal reflection. How-to and self-help books will prove superficial when it comes to finding religious truth for one's maturing years.

A Gospel for the Mature Years is different. It offers a dozen provocative chapters that guide the reader to a deepening committment to God. More than that, it provides inspiration for the facing of whatever may come as one experiences declining energy and health, and other diminished powers and resources.

There are two lists in the book that make it a reference worth keeping at hand, especially on gloomy or discouraging days. The first list lays out all the key human needs that people face as children of God. The second describes all the many gifts people can share freely with others. The lists are fleshed out with highly readable anecdotes about real people.

The authors–a psychiatrist and a retired clergyman and his wife–genuinely believe that no human being who is still breathing is without a gift to share. Discovering what our gifts are during the changing seasons of our lives is accomplished through interaction with other human beings and through prayer. These writers carefully avoid a simple doffing of their hats to religious truth; they regard a relationship with God as a positively essential aspect of full humanity.

Questions at the end of each chapter will serve either an individual reader or a discussion group at church or elsewhere."

Locke E. Bowman, Jr., LHD
Professor Emeritus of Christian
Education and Pastoral Theology,
Virginia Theological Seminary

More pre-publication
REVIEWS, COMMENTARIES, EVALUATIONS . . .

"Since the 1940s, a great sea of material has been generated about the needs, concerns, and desires of older adults. There is even a plethora of self-help material for older adults, themselves, to address the aging journey. But within this vast body of material, there is a desert, a vacant space where the spiritual needs of older adults have not been included within this literary bonanza. The new book, *A Gospel for the Mature Years,* finds a home in this desolation.

I was excited to receive an advanced copy of this new text. Harold Koenig and his colleagues are to be congratulated for conceptualizing and bringing to the public a challenging and thoughtful new text. It takes some courage in the current literary environment to begin with definitions of terms that philosophers and authors have struggled for centuries to define. Yet, by doing so, the reader begins to grasp the parameters of the task. The succeeding chapters then help readers to continue to articulate their spiritual journey. The gift of this text is that it offers many guidelines, but never a fixed road, allowing the readers to define much of the geography.

A Gospel for the Mature Years should be a welcome addition to the resource libraries of every Christian educator and lay leader who works with adults and seniors. I highly recommend it."

James W. Ellor, DMin, LCSW
Professor of Gerontology
and Human Services,
National-Louis University,
Wheaton, Illinois

"As we grow older, eyesight may fail us, but this book offers us another 'vision' of how life can be in later years. The authors are practical in their outlook, gracing us with stories of people who use their God-given gifts for others. The only reason older adults should use a rocking chair is to read this book; otherwise, give the chair and book to someone else and begin to put your talents and gifts to work in service to others."

Roger Prehn, MDiv
Pastor, St. Paul's Lutheran Church,
Durham, North Carolina

"**T**his book offers a very practical guide for traditional Christians to think about and apply their faith in outreaching ways during the later years. Drawing upon his years as a geriatric psychiatrist, Harold Koenig offers a basic course in Christian piety that will speak the language of many older Christians. With the aid of longtime church leaders Tracy and Betty Lamar, Dr. Koenig describes in understandable terms some twenty-five needs persons have, needs toward self, God, and others.

Building upon an active Christian lifestyle image, the authors discuss the use of talents to serve others. A telling remark reflecting the faith ideology of the book states: 'We believe that every person at every age, in every circumstance, has a unique talent, ability, or gift that at least partly explains why he or she is in that situation.' The discussion about talents changing over the years represents a very helpful image in light of the changing society and changing opportunities persons face over the decades. The authors optimistically identify nearly fifty different talents that people have in later years, ranging from emotional, to spiritual, to instrumental ones.

This book would serve middle-age persons beginning to shape retirement ideas well, but could probably be valuable reading for any adult Christian desiring to evolve a lifestyle of what John Wesley years ago called 'practical Christianity.' The book should be an excellent resource for congregational groups of all denominations among adult groups of all ages."

James J. Seeber, PhD
Associate Director,
Center for Aging,
Religion, and Spirituality,
Luther Seminary,
St. Paul, Minnesota

"**T**he authors clearly grasp this central truth of the second half of life: God has a purpose for us and we are integral to God's vision for a just and compassionate world. Step-by-step they lead us–individually and in study groups–to a balanced but passionate commitment to making a difference and, in that, experiencing satisfaction and joy in our mature years."

Henry C. Simmons, PhD
Professor of Religion and Aging,
Presbyterian School
of Christian Education,
Richmond, Virginia

More pre-publication
REVIEWS, COMMENTARIES, EVALUATIONS . . .

"**T**his masterful biblically researched work as well as practical application gives the senior Christian a path and/or vision of how the later years of life can be the best. One must be willing to commit oneself to the two commandments of loving God and neighbor as self.

The book will have a broad appeal to all Christian denominations. It is easy to read. It will be valuable to one's private meditation and growth as well as in small group study. The questions for discussion at the end of each chapter are most insightful."

Richard M. Slyman, DMin
Pastor, First Presbyterian Church,
Port Richie, Florida

"**A** *Gospel for the Mature Years* by Harold G. Koenig with Tracy and Betty Lamar is packed with insightful perspectives on how to attain total well-being in later life. It is clearly based upon the Judeo-Christian Scriptures as the ultimate authority, but it also reflects the senior author's psychiatric expertise in its practical advice on how to attain mental and spiritual health and fulfillment. It is a good text for discussion groups and adult religious education as well as a resource for personal inspiration and study."

Dr. David O. Moberg
Professor of Sociology,
Marquette University,
Milwaukee, Wisconsin

The Haworth Pastoral Press
An Imprint of The Haworth Press, Inc.

A Gospel
for the Mature Years
Finding Fulfillment
by Knowing and Using
Your Gifts

HAWORTH Religion and Mental Health
Harold G. Koenig, MD
Senior Editor

A Gospel for the Mature Years: Finding Fulfillment by Knowing and Using Your Gifts by Harold Koenig, Tracy Lamar, and Betty Lamar

Is Religion Good for Your Health? The Effects of Religion on Physical and Mental Health by Harold Koenig

Additional Titles of Related Interest:

Growing Up: Pastoral Nurture for the Later Years by Thomas B. Robb

Religion and the Family: When God Helps by Laurel Arthur Burton

Victims of Dementia: Services, Support, and Care by Wm. Michael Clemmer

Horrific Traumata: A Pastoral Response to the Post-Traumatic Stress Disorder by N. Duncan Sinclair

Aging and God: Spiritual Pathways to Mental Health in Midlife and Later Years by Harold G. Koenig

Counseling for Spiritually Empowered Wholeness: A Hope-Centered Approach by Howard Clinebell

Shame: A Faith Perspective by Robert H. Albers

Dealing with Depression: Five Pastoral Interventions by Richard Dayringer

Righteous Religion: Unmasking the Illusions of Fundamentalism and Authoritarian Catholicism by Kathleen Y. Ritter and Craig W. O'Neill

Theological Context for Pastoral Caregiving: Word in Deed by Howard Stone

Pastoral Care in Pregnancy Loss: A Ministry Long Needed by Thomas Moe

The Soul in Distress: What Every Pastoral Counselor Should Know About Emotional and Mental Illness by Richard Roukema

A Gospel for the Mature Years

Finding Fulfillment by Knowing and Using Your Gifts

Harold G. Koenig, MD
with
Tracy Lamar, MDiv
and Betty Lamar, BFA

The Haworth Pastoral Press
An Imprint of The Haworth Press, Inc.
New York • London

Published by

The Haworth Pastoral Press, an imprint of The Haworth Press, Inc., 10 Alice Street, Binghamton, NY 13904-1580

Cover design by Donna M. Brooks.

Library of Congress Cataloging-in-Publication Data

Koenig, Harold George.
    A gospel for the mature years : finding fulfillment by knowing and using your gifts / Harold G. Koenig : with Tracy Lamar and Betty Lamar.
        p.   cm.
    Includes bibliographical references and index.
    ISBN 0-7890-0170-5 (alk. paper).
    1. Middle aged persons–Religious life. 2. Aged–Religious life. 3. Christian life. I. Lamar, Tracy. II. Lamar, Betty.
III. Title.
BV4579.5K64   1997
248.8'5–dc21
                                                        96-46279
                                                        CIP

To my mother, Maria Koenig, on her eighty-first birthday.

ABOUT THE AUTHORS

Harold G. Koenig, MD, completed his undergraduate education at Stanford University, his medical school training at the University of California at San Francisco, and his geriatric medicine and psychiatry training at Duke University Medical Center. He is currently on the faculty of Duke as an Associate Professor of Psychiatry and Behavioral Sciences and an Assistant Professor of Internal Medicine, and is Director of the Program on Religion, Aging, and Health at that institution. Dr. Koenig has published over 100 scientific articles and book chapters as well as seven books; his research on religion and health has been featured on National Public Radio, *ABC World News Tonight, CBS This Morning, NBC Evening News,* Ivanhoe Broadcast News, *Arthritis Today,* the *Daily Telegraph* (London), the *Guardian* (Europe), and numerous other national and international programs and news reports. He was one of the conveners of a conference sponsored by the National Institute on Aging on the topic of "Religion, Aging, and Health," and he recently organized a symposium on religion and health at the American Association for the Advancement of Science, the largest science organization in the world. He is the recipient of a five-year Mental Health Academic Award from the National Institute of Mental Health to study depression in older persons with medical illness.

Tracy Lamar, MDiv, has been a Priest of the Episcopal Church for some fifty-four years. With the exception of his years as a Navy chaplain in World War II, he has served his time as a Parish Priest. Now retired, he and his wife Betty are residents of The Forest at Duke retirement community in Durham. At present, he is serving on the Committee for Aging of the Episcopal Diocese of North Carolina.

Betty Lamar, BFA, an active lifetime member of the Episcopal Church, was deeply involved with her first husband in the Church's renewal "Faith Alive" for a number of years. Through this and other activities, she has been involved in the experience, training, and conduct of small group programs in the Church. It has been with this background that she has prepared the materials for this book for use in small church groups. Betty also serves on the Committee for Aging, Diocese of North Carolina.

CONTENTS

Foreword

In the book of Genesis it is recorded that God created human life, male and female, and pronounced the event was very good. There was no suggestion that the warranty on "the very good" expired at age sixty-five. It might seem a bit presumptuous to ask what God had in mind for the later years of life. Chances are, life would look something like Harold Koenig's description of *A Gospel for the Mature Years*, in which the needs of persons are fulfilled by discovering their gifts and talents to serve others.

The common view of aging thirty years ago, when I included an intentional ministry with older adults in my pastoral opportunities, declared that life topped out early and then slid downhill to the end. Age thirty was thought to be the zenith of life, reinforced with the warning "Don't trust anyone over thirty." Despite the experience of most older persons and supporting research to the contrary, this myth still persists today.

Most people are enjoying twenty-five to thirty-five years after retirement from their workplace with the possibility of living creative and meaningful lives. Instead of topping out at age thirty, they are reporting that the peak years of their lives are in the sixties, seventies, eighties, and even nineties. Chronological age doesn't have much to do with the time when life really comes together and individuals begin to feel good about themselves and their contributions to life. That period of achievement relates more to personal health, stimulation, imagination, experience, and the connections we are able to make with God, neighbor, and self. This is what Koenig is helping us to see in this book.

When the first Shepherd's Center was formed by the twenty-five cooperating interfaith congregations in Kansas City, Missouri in 1972, older adults were concerned about maintaining an independent lifestyle. People spoke of avoiding life in a nursing home as if everyone was headed full speed into one. This was necessary for 4.6 percent of those over age sixty-five, but not the other 95 percent. The proportion of persons over age sixty-five who reside in nursing homes has not changed in nearly three decades.The number of residents has increased with the population but the percentage has remained the same–4.6 percent. We realized that about one-third of those in care centers could live in more independent settings if families or society could make arrangements. The concern of older adults in the 1970s focused on independence.

In the 1980s the focus shifted to concerns for life enrichment or quality of life. People wanted to live as long as possible but only as long as life offered opportunities for enrichment. The 1980s witnessed an explosion of learning for older adults with the advent of Elderhostels, which have grown rapidly to involve nearly 800,000 participants today. Universities, colleges, community cultural groups, and many older persons themselves have given verbal endorsement to such involvement, as has the research literature that emphasizes quality of life.

Shepherd's Centers of America (now with nearly one hundred centers in twenty-six states) anticipated the desire for older adults to engage in lifelong learning from the beginning in 1972. We developed an exciting education-socialization model named "Adventures in Learning" that was unlike freestanding classes, taught by paid teachers, with a set course of classes. Adventures in Learning is a freer model with exciting topics representing subject matter for the head, hand, heart, and health. Quarter terms are fashioned with the option of three to ten classes to choose from between each hour, conducted one day each week, taught by qualified volunteer leaders/teachers, with the classes held in congregation facilities. Adventures in Learning is a model in which older volunteers manage the whole enterprise. In the 1980s, older adults were not satisfied just to live a long time, even independently. Life was measured by the joy, the excitement, and the stimulation, all of which contributed to a quality life.

In the 1990s, the primary concern for older adults shifted to *giving*, as well as receiving. The loud cry of the decade has been "Who needs me?" The common concern has been to wake up in the morning with a feeling that some person or some cause is waiting for your hands and your mind. Older adults have drawn much of their life satisfaction from their careers and their work. The task of the 1990s has been to find volunteer opportunities that approach a new sense of vocation. It is the gift of self today to persons and causes that promises to make a difference to the future. Older persons of this decade search to be reassured that they are wanted and needed. Being wanted and needed has given hope and purpose to this new generation of older adults who were tempted to feel that society had discarded them.

Koenig has a message of reassurance to all older adults as he explores how wonderful it is to discover one's gifts, to help others discover their gifts, and then dedicate one's self to helping others. Jesus at the beginning of his work went out into the wilderness in search of an understanding of his mission. He became hungry on his journey and was taunted to turn stones into bread to feed himself. He refused to pervert his authority and power for that purpose. In my forty-seven-year career as a parish minister, I have met a few frauds and fakes along the way, but I have never met anyone who tried to turn stone into bread. Unfortunately, I have met a multitude of people who misunderstood the possibilities of life in their later years. Not realizing that God's warranty of "very good" has not expired, they have taken the bread of life and turned it into stone. How easy it is to miss what God surely intended for the later years of our lives until we are challenged by the options of *A Gospel for the Mature Years*.

Elbert C. Cole, ThD

Acknowledgments

We the authors would like to express our sincere appreciation to Dr. Andrew Weaver and Dr. Keith Meador for the many hours they spent reading over this manuscript and providing us with their insightful comments. Also, a thanks to Pastor Ron Lewis, whose inspiring life and teachings have directly contributed to this work. In particular, we would like to thank our dear friend and colleague, Dr. David Moberg, for his extraordinarily detailed line-by-line review and editing of this book.

Chapter 1

About This Book

Neglect not the gift that is in thee.

—Timothy 4:14, KJV*

A Gospel for the Mature Years is "good news" for those desiring
spiritual and emotional growth in the years past middle age. We
have written this book for people who are seeking spiritual maturity, well-being, and purpose for their lives now and are looking
forward to useful and meaningful years of retirement ahead. We
hope the "good news" contained in this book will give you a vision
that will make the second half of your life even more fulfilling than
the first. We do not believe that these years were meant to be a time
for idleness and withdrawal from life, nor a time of waiting for life's
end or trying to stay busy to avoid boredom. No, we believe that
this should be an exciting, meaningful, action-packed time when we
should grab hold of life and live it fully, advancing God's kingdom
in our families, communities, and nation.

These are increasingly difficult times requiring that God's people
work together, utilizing their talents for the benefit of others, and
ultimately for their own. Rising crime, political corruption, poverty,
drug and alcohol use, a young generation with no vision, purpose,

---

*Unless otherwise indicated, all Biblical quotes are from the New International
Standard version (NIV). Quotes from the King James (KJV), the American Standard (ASV), the Revised Standard (RSV), or the Living Bible (LB) are also used,
depending on the translation that best expresses a point. Portions of some quotes
have been italicized by the authors for emphasis. We liberally quote and reference
Scripture throughout this book. These Scripture references are examples of biblical
teachings, and are not intended to be "prooftexts" in the narrow, negative sense of
the word.

1

or hope–this is the direction our nation is heading. We believe that developing a deep, personal, intimate relationship with God and then serving our Creator diligently by serving others can help the Christian achieve joy and fulfillment during these turbulent times. The call to relationship and to service does not end with retirement, with sickness, nor even when a person becomes totally disabled and dependent on others for physical needs. In every one of these situations God has given us a unique and special gift. Our job is to find out what this gift, talent, or ability is, and then use it to serve.

This does not mean that there are never times when we must "be still before the Lord" (Psalm 37:7, 46:10) and cease from busy-ness and activity. As we grow older, there is an increasing need to become more contemplative. The spiritual life is often a waiting for the unfolding. This is indeed the receptive-female side of God that cannot be ignored or devalued. We are not encouraging you to make *activity* your Idol. Nor do we advocate salvation by "works," for we believe that it is only by faith in Christ that we are ultimately saved and that there is nothing more we can do that Christ has not already done. It is possible, however, to be loved, accepted, and saved by Christ, and yet still be unhappy and unfulfilled during our life here on earth. We believe that the Bible provides vital information not only on how to grow spiritually, but also on how to achieve mental health. This involves balancing "being" with "acting" and "enjoying" with "serving."

Helping middle-aged and older adults overcome spiritual and emotional problems has been the focus of our work for many years. The Reverend Mr. Lamar and his wife Betty have been involved in pastoral ministry for over fifty years, working at the local congregational level and at the state level. Dr. Koenig has worked in clinical practice both as a family physician and as a psychiatrist for the past two decades. Both his clinical experience with patients and the results of over ten major research studies he has led at Duke University Medical Center have confirmed the truth of what the Bible says about how to live a full and satisfying life.[1] During these years of ministry, research, and our own aging, we have learned some important information–we think *Good News*–that will help you achieve a satisfying, meaningful, and joy-filled life.

The years past middle age bring special psychological and spiritual needs, needs that we think can be met by applying simple but widely known biblical principles whose truth has been repeatedly tested in the crucible of time. The ideas presented here are firmly rooted in Judeo-Christian scriptures and should be acceptable to persons from a wide range of Christian backgrounds. We realize and hope that you will not agree with everything written here, so we encourage you to give feedback by writing to us about your experiences, ideas, and reactions; we, too, are growing in our understanding of these things and need your help (Box 3400, Duke University Medical Center, Durham, North Carolina 27710).

The Vision.[2] As persons move into and through middle age, they increasingly experience a need to contribute to the welfare of the generations that will follow them. The desire to acquire things for themselves slowly weakens as they begin to feel the need to invest in the future of others—their children, grandchildren, and younger persons in society. What aging persons fear the most is that they will be a burden to others, that their lives will lose meaning and usefulness. They fear that they will die before having a chance to make life better for those who remain behind, and instead perhaps even make life worse for them. Already, aging adults are beginning to feel guilty because of the financial burden they are placing on younger persons who will be spending more and more of their paychecks to keep social programs such as Medicare and social security solvent in the years ahead. Rather than ensuring the welfare and happiness of the future generations, we find ourselves draining society of its increasingly scarce resources. More than ever, this creates a need within us to examine our usefulness and seek out ways that we can contribute to the betterment of society in the years to come.

We firmly believe that middle-aged and older adults are living in a critical time when *more than ever before* we have an *opportunity to impact in a positive way* on the generations that follow us. Our youth are seeking direction, seeking hope, seeking for something that will give their lives stability, meaning, depth, character. They are searching for role models of people whose lives demonstrate these qualities. They are tired of striving endlessly for the superficial pleasures of materialism. They feel empty and unfulfilled by the "things" that previous generations valued so highly. They want something more, but they do not know what that something is. Many have lost hope of ever finding it and have become cynical as a result.

Our generation can act as a catalyst to the generations to come to produce a society of people with vision—a vision of hope that their lives can have meaning and purpose regardless of circumstances, and of faith that every person has been given a gift by God that will enable them to make a difference in this world and make it a better place for their children and grandchildren. Here is the game plan.

The Two Great Commandments. We will focus on the two principles that we believe undergird all Judeo-Christian scriptures and form a firm basis for spiritual and emotional health. One day a Pharisee asked Jesus, testing him, "Teacher, which is the greatest commandment in the Law?" (Matthew 22:36). Jesus replied, quoting the sixth chapter of Deuteronomy, verse 5, " '*Love the Lord your God with all your heart and with all your soul and with all your strength.*' This is the first and greatest commandment." He then followed quickly with a quotation from the nineteenth chapter of Leviticus, verse 18: "And the second [commandment] is like it: '*Love your neighbor as yourself.*' " Commenting on what he just said, Jesus adds: "All the Law and the Prophets hang on these two commandments." The Living Bible's wording is "Keep only these and you will find that you are obeying all the others."

Most of us have read and reread these scriptures often, perhaps hundreds of times. To some of us, they have lost their meaning and impact—like the sound of pounding waves on the seashore that has become hardly noticeable to those who live nearby. To others, these directives seem unrealistic, impossible to fulfill. We have our reasons, however, for making these two commandments the focus of this book. These two principles are emphasized throughout scripture, both Old and New Testaments. The Ten Commandments in the Old Testament rest firmly on them—the first four dealing with our relationship to God and the remaining six addressing our relationships to people. Most important, in the New Testament Jesus instructs us that these principles should be the foundations on which we build our lives. Third, and least important though significant, is that recent scientific research is discovering that these two elements of faith are vital for mental health in persons at any age.[3]

In the pages ahead, we will show how both spiritual and mental health are closely related to the extent that we implement these two principles in daily life.[4] Chapters 6 through 10 focus almost entirely on these commandments. We hope, however, that you will see their imprints on every page of this book as we help you to think about where you are now, where you would like to go, and how you are going to get there.

REASON FOR AND DESIGN OF THIS STUDY GUIDE

There are few resources within either the religious community or the medical community that address the unique spiritual and emotional needs of persons in middle age and later life. In both of these disciplines, it is assumed that preparation for the "later years" has already been accomplished by this time in life. In the religious community, the older generation is supposed to be content with attending church services and social functions like church suppers, helping with church bazaars, or doing a little volunteer busy work. In the medical community, the concern for spiritual welfare and growth is discounted as either irrelevant or maladaptive. These views neglect the particular circumstances, as well as the spiritual and emotional needs with which persons past middle-age must grapple— changes in lifestyle, changes in personal identity, threatening health and financial circumstances, and increasingly pressing questions about life's purpose and meaning.

We ask you to explore with us five major questions. First, we ask, in the form of self-examination, "Where are we in our spiritual growth?" Much like a physical examination, we seek a diagnosis for our spiritual health. Related to this is the question, "Where are we going?" We recognize that each of us is at a unique place in our spiritual pilgrimage. There must, however, be some common goal for which we are heading. Knowing this goal or goals will give us a vision and help keep us on the right path to achieve it. Third, in the light of this self-examination, we ask "What is ahead for us?" We face possible changes in circumstances as we age. What are these changes and how can we deal with them? Fourth, after examining our current condition and anticipating changing circumstances, we inquire "What will our needs be?" In other words, what are the specific spiritual and emotional needs of middle-aged and older persons? Finally, "What can we do to meet these needs?" We want a scripture-based plan to meet our needs now and prepare us to face the challenges that will confront us in the future.

As noted before, the basis for our exploration and study is Judeo-Christian Scripture, and in particular, the life, teachings, and example of Jesus Christ. Our goal is to direct, motivate, and inspire you to develop a deeper knowledge and experience of God so that you can live life to the fullest, as you love and serve those "neighbors" with whom the Lord has surrounded you.

WHERE ARE WE NOW AND WHERE ARE WE GOING?

Where we are now involves both our relationship with God and our relationships with others in the Christian community. First, where am I in terms of my relationship with God? Do I really believe there is a God? Do I experience God in any type of meaningful way in my daily life? Is God the focus of my ultimate concern, and if not, what is? How much effort am I willing to expend to achieve growth in this area? How much do I desire spiritual growth? How much do I need spiritual growth? We ask similar questions of our relationships within the Christian community. What does being part of Christ's church mean to me? Why do I belong to a community of believers? How and to what extent am I sharing in the spiritual life of others in my church and helping to shoulder the burdens of those in need?

Having located where we are now, we ask where are we going. Do we have a goal and vision for our spiritual life? Here we explore the characteristics of the maturing Christian, again in terms of our relationship with God and relationships with others. We set goals, realizing that achieving them may not be possible in this life, but knowing that their sincere pursuit will lead us closer and closer to God's plan for our lives and to the fruits thereof—"love, joy, peace, patience, kindness, goodness, faithfulness, gentleness and self-control" (Galatians 5:22-23). Jesus said, "For the gate is small, and the way is narrow that leads to life, and few are those who find it . . .

You will know them by their fruits" (Matthew 7:14,16, ASV). This fruit is both for us and for our children and grandchildren.

WHAT IS AHEAD FOR US?

This is called a transition question. Many of us are beginning to face change. For some, this involves a transition from the discipline of work to the leisure of retirement. For others it involves a transition from a household of children to the "empty nest." For still others, from feelings of security about finances, health, and living conditions, to unknown circumstances. When anticipating retirement, we often think longingly: "When I retire . . . !" However, when the distractions of travel, golf, fishing, and other leisure activities wear off, then what? The question, "What will I do now?" often reflects boredom, unrest, and perhaps a sense of unfulfillment with the shallowness of these activities. "What will I do?" is quickly followed by the more difficult question "Who will I be?" While it is important to learn that just "being" is OK, we are always in the process of "doing." Even just "being" takes a lot of doing. We obtain much of our sense of self and self-esteem from what we do. If what we are doing is not providing purpose or meaning to our lives, then we should be open to other possibilities. Trying to justify why our lives are meaningful and useful, when in reality they are not, is not helpful.

WHAT WILL OUR NEEDS BE?

As we move into this second half of life, the circumstances and living conditions of each of us will vary. Some of us will remain in our homes. Others will move to retirement communities or nursing homes. Some will be blessed with affluence. Others will struggle with limited resources and finances. Accepting these varied conditions, all will share certain basic psychological and spiritual needs. As we explore and come to understand what these needs are, we will be better prepared to meet them effectively in the days ahead and, thus, to age successfully and live fully, regardless of our circumstances.

HOW DO WE MEET THESE NEEDS?

The fulfillment of all psychological and spiritual needs, we believe, follows as a direct result of living out the two great commandments of loving God and loving neighbor. In short, this is accomplished by: (1) coming into a close, deep, and meaningful relationship with God; (2) hearing God's call to serve; (3) discovering our unique and special gift, ability, or talent that God has given us; and (4) through God's grace, using that talent to serve our Creator by serving others. It's that simple. Easy to understand, but quite difficult to carry out, as most of us know. In this book, we will discuss how to develop a deeper relationship with and experience of God and, in the process, become aware of God's grace and calling in our lives for this time and age. We will describe how to go about identifying our special talents, given each of our unique life circumstances. Finally, we will discuss how loving and serving God by serving others can give our lives meaning, purpose, and usefulness, and help meet our deepest psychological and spiritual needs.

AVOIDING EXTREMES AND BURNOUT

This section is one of the most important parts of the book. Much of what we are saying requires *balance*. "Using your gift" may be taken to the extreme–a compulsive overactivity driven by unhealthy guilt or an emphasis on "works." You must avoid such excesses and extremes. Indeed, the "way is narrow that leads to life," and many traps await the unwary pilgrim. There is a very real spiritual force that does not want us to serve God, love our neighbor, or lead powerful and exemplary Christian lives. If you are not cautious, you can find yourself serving others in the wrong manner and for the wrong reasons. This can and will bring about disappointment, bitterness, despair, exhaustion, and burnout. Many people want to love and serve others, but they simply do not know how to do this without getting overwhelmed or burned out in the process. Because we as therapists have encountered these same problems ourselves and have seen them repeatedly in others, we have some ideas about what the traps are and how to avoid them.

SMALL GROUP DISCUSSION AND SHARING

This book is meant both for individual reading and for use in churches as a workbook for small discussion groups. It is ideal for Bible study groups, home "cell" groups, and adult Sunday school, and has been divided into twelve chapters so it can be used for classes running on a calendar quarter of thirteen Sundays. Questions for discussion and sharing by the group have been placed at the end of each chapter. These questions have been designed to encourage individual preparation for participation in the group. Using the subject of the chapter to be discussed, each member of the group should be committed to study and preparation for each session.

The life of the group will be enriched if the leadership is shared by members of the group. The leader should be willing to share his or her experiences, feelings, and reactions to the discussion questions, and encourage other members to share theirs as well. Each member should assume a responsibility for discussion and sharing. The leader might consider starting each meeting with a prayer and time for reflection on the material presented in the chapter, as an introduction to discussion and sharing. Time should be allowed at the conclusion of each session for the answering of questions that members may have.

The members of the group should determine the number of sessions (ideally twelve) with an agreed upon time, place, and length for each session. In order that the members of the group may form a caring and trusting community, it is best that no additions be made to the group until the agreed upon number of sessions have been completed and that each original member commit to attend all sessions. Finally, it is absolutely essential that confidentiality be maintained by all members of the group; in other words, things that are said in the group should go no further than the persons in the group.

SUMMARY

This book is written for middle-aged and older adults who wish to grow emotionally and spiritually, and experience satisfaction and joy in their mature years. The "good news" is that this is possible regardless of our circumstances, health, or age. The reader will be given a Vision that is full of hope and firmly rooted in reality. This reality is based upon promises in scripture and on the two great commandments of loving God and loving neighbor, whose benefits are increasingly being confirmed by medical science. In the chapters ahead we will be asking ourselves "Where are we now?"; "Where are we going?"; and "What is ahead for us?" We will then look at our psychological and spiritual needs and discuss how we can best meet those needs by knowing and using our gifts. Chapter 11 is particularly important because it examines how to avoid burnout and exhaustion when loving and serving others. This book is meant both for individual reading and for use in small discussion groups, and has questions at the end of each chapter to stimulate discussion.

DISCUSSION QUESTIONS

1. What does the word "gospel" mean to you?
2. What about the word "vision?" Discuss what it means to have a vision, and why this might be helpful for emotional and spiritual growth.
3. According to Jesus in Matthew 22:36, which is the greatest commandment? How is the second greatest commandment related to the first?
4. What are three things you hope to get from reading this book? What are three things you hope to get from participating in this group? Write these down.
5. What are the "ground rules" for your group (if rules are used in group setting)?

NOTES

1. Koenig, Harold G. *Is Religion Good for Your Health? The Effects of Religion on Physical and Mental Health.* Binghamton, NY: The Haworth Press, 1997.

2. The authors would like to express thanks to Dr. Elbert Cole for his help in developing this section.

3. Koenig, Harold G. *Research on Religion and Aging.* Westport, CT: Greenwood Press, 1995.

4. There is really a third principle that we assume, but emphasize in Chapter 11. That principle is care for self. Jesus said, "Love your neighbor *as yourself.*" You will have a difficult time loving and serving others unless you love, respect, and care for yourself.

Chapter 2

Definition of Terms

In order to discuss our topic meaningfully, we must clarify what we mean by the terms we use. These definitions are important because words can have many different meanings to people from different backgrounds. For example, religion can mean "attending church services" to one person, "a personal belief in God" to another, "helping one's neighbor" to a third, and "coming into contact with nature" to a fourth. We will define our terms clearly and specifically, yet broadly enough to accommodate a wide range of Judeo-Christian beliefs. This will provide us with a common language. As you consider these definitions in your discussion groups, you may elaborate on or modify them to fit your own goals better. If you choose to use these terms in ways other than defined here, however, we encourage you to acknowledge this and come to an agreement on a common definition in your group.

AGING SUCCESSFULLY

We understand aging as the process of growing older that begins with birth and ends with death, encompassing physical, psychological, and spiritual changes that take place throughout the life cycle. "Successful" aging does not mean success merely in terms of good physical health, financial security, or the fulfillment of career or social goals. Instead, our definition of successful aging focuses on how people deal with "crises" in their lives, overcome threatening life circumstances, solve problems, and make difficult but morally sound decisions, factors that often have nothing to do with physical or material circumstances. This type of "success" depends on how we perceive and respond to the events in our lives.

MENTAL HEALTH

This term describes a wide range of mental functioning, from mental illness to normal or ordinary psychological health, to extraordinary adaptive and robust living. The healthy mental state is characterized by freedom from fear, anxiety, and the entanglements of resentment, greed, envy, and jealousy. It is marked by the ability to form stable, fulfilling, and intimate relationships, i.e., the capacity to focus on and invest oneself in the lives of others. This capacity may be defined as the process of loving. Mental health, then, involves the capacity to freely give and receive love.

GOD

We believe in the Christian God who is the Creator and sustainer of all life. God is our Savior in Jesus Christ in whom God became one of us, and the Holy Spirit is our constant counselor and guide. God is as distant from us as the furthermost galaxies and as close to us as the "breath we breathe." God is personal. God knows our name, and as St. Augustine declares, "Loves each of us as if we were the only one in creation." God runs out to meet the prodigal son. We are always being invited home by God. More than that, God runs out to find us. In the parable of the lost sheep, God leaves the ninety-nine seeking the one—you and me. God's generosity is the heart of the mystery. It is almost impossible to believe. We think of God as reflected in great persons such as St. Francis ministering to the lepers or Jesus with the little children—compassionate, tender, merciful. We believe that God is interested in and wants to be involved in our lives and, in fact, has a very definite plan for each of us.

We see God as having both female and male traits—a receptive, contemplative side, and an active, more aggressive side. We try to convey this in our use of language. The Bible has many female images for God. For instance, Proverbs 1:20: "Wisdom calls aloud in the streets, *she* raises *her* voice in the public squares." Consider Isaiah 42:14 where the Lord is portrayed "like a woman in childbirth, I cry out . . . " Female images are seen even in the Gospels: "How often I have longed to gather your children together, as a hen gathers her chicks under her wings" (Matthew 23:37; also Luke 13:34).

CHRISTIAN

We are not using the term "Christian" as it is typically used today, i.e., any person affiliated with or a member of a Protestant or Catholic denomination, someone who regularly attends a Christian church, or someone who prays and reads the Bible regularly. Being a Christian involves both belief and action. Christian, as we use it, describes a person who: (1) believes that Christ was God incarnate (God become human); (2) believes that Christ died for our sins; (3) believes that Christ arose from the dead and is our hope of salvation; and (4) is *trying to live* in a way that reflects the life and teachings of Jesus Christ. How did Jesus say that others would recognize us as Christians? "By this all men will know that you are my disciples, if you love one another" (John 13:35; see also James 2:26). Not by the church we are affiliated with, not by going to church regularly, not even by having a consistent devotional time, but *by our love for one another.*

BIBLE

The Holy Bible is composed of the Old and New Testaments. We believe that the Bible was inspired by God, and that all of it is useful for understanding who God is, what God is like, and how we can best serve our Creator. This use of scripture follows directly from Paul's letter to Timothy, "All scripture is inspired by God and profitable for teaching, for reproof, for correction and for training in righteousness, that the man [or woman] of God may be complete, equipped for every good work" (2 Timothy 3:16-17, RSV). We use the Bible as our primary reference and final authority for the advice and direction contained in this book. As Abraham Lincoln once wrote, "I am profitably engaged in reading the Bible. Take all of this Book upon reason that you can, and the balance upon faith. You will live and die a better man."

RELIGION

The term "religion" is usually defined as the outward and visible signs of faith in a person's life. It includes traditional activities such as prayer or meditation, scripture reading, attendance at church, participation in the sacraments, and so forth. Religion has both doctrinal and mystical elements. Doctrinal elements involve the teachings, including laws and rules, of the church. Mystical elements include contemplation, meditation, intuition, mystery, and communion with God outside of human reason. Religion is described in scripture in terms of action or "doing." According to the apostle James, "Religion that is pure and undefiled before God and the Father is this: to visit orphans and widows in their affliction, and to keep oneself unstained from the world" (James 1:27, RSV). Religion is often distinguished from "spirituality."

SPIRITUALITY

This term has unfortunately become popularized to the point that it can involve almost any type of human experience or identification. Nature, music, or great works of art can convey spiritual experiences, with or without acknowledging God. This makes a universally acceptable definition almost impossible. Many people who cannot admit to being religious, will readily agree that they are "spiritual." The central intended purpose of Christian religious rituals, institutions, and activities is the awakening, nurturing, and deepening of the human spirit in order to convey and nourish spiritual life. Spirituality refers to that part of the person that is neither body nor mind, not tethered to the material universe. The Spirit is that divine and immortal aspect of God that each of us shares with the Creator as people created in God's image. This represents our true identity. We *have* a mind. We *have* a body. We do not have a spirit; we *are* Spirit. The Spirit is what distinguishes humans from all animals and all other parts of creation. It provides us with the capacity to seek, experience, and commune with God. Other definitions of spirituality do not distinguish or separate spirit from the body or mind, but see it as overlapping with and including both of those human dimensions.

FAITH

Faith is believing without seeing. It is being "sure of what we hope for and certain of what we do not see" (Hebrews 11:1). Faith has both *structure* and *content*. Faith as "structure" is the act or process of believing in or having confidence in something. According to Paul Tillich, faith is the act or process of making *something* the object of our "ultimate concern."[1] The "content" of faith, on the other hand, is what that *something* is. According to James Fowler, the content of faith may be either religious or nonreligious in nature.[2] In this book, we are not interested so much in the structure of faith as in its content. The content of our faith is religious in nature and involves the knowledge of, understanding of, and adherence to the life and teachings of Jesus Christ. The content and focus of our ultimate concern is centered on the revelation of God in Christ (Colossians 2:6). This content of faith–as opposed to self, another person, work, pleasure, possessions, institution, or social group–is what we commit our trust and highest level of allegiance to.

We believe that it is the *content* of faith, rather than simply its form (i.e., faith in anything), that determines the effects that faith will have on mental health and well-being. "What we believe" makes a difference. People place their faith in many things other than God. The ultimate concern of an alcoholic may be from where his or her next drink will come. The object of the alcoholic's faith is acquiring alcohol. For the business-person, making money may be the ultimate concern. For a person in love, the lover may become the focus of their faith. These "contents" of faith here described are very different from a focus on a personal relationship with God in the revelation of Jesus Christ.

This view is consistent with the first commandment which states "Thou shalt have no other gods before me" (Exodus 20:3, KJV).

We believe that it was with good reason that God made this the first commandment. Our Creator knew that failure to follow it would have devastating effects on our spiritual, emotional, and physical health. Anything besides God that we allow to become an idol in our lives will rule over and control us.

GRACE

Grace is the unconditional, unbounded love of God. We are loved by God without reservation. We have to do absolutely nothing to be constantly loved by God. Our natural response to such love is thanksgiving and gratitude and generosity. As we recognize and respond to God's grace, we will *start wanting* to live a more generous and gracious life. God in Christ died for us so that we can triumph over sin and death and live for eternity with God some day. God accepts us, loves us, and wants to be a part of our lives–this is grace. Because grace is a free gift to all, there is no earned credit in doing good. Instead, we seek to do good as a natural response to God's generosity toward us. If we could earn God's favor, we might have grounds to believe we are better than others. Grace is God's radical, free gift of unmerited acceptance that allows no ground for self-righteousness.

Humility, the acknowledgement and understanding of our sinful nature, is what enables us to recognize God's grace in our lives and to experience the thankfulness that follows such a realization. The truth of the matter is that we have done nothing and cannot do anything to warrant God's love. It is by grace that God loves us and saves us (1 Corinthians 15:10). We believe that all of our spiritual progress is ultimately a direct result of God's grace. In all the trials and tribulations, doubts and wonders of life, Christian faith has always assured the believer that God goes before us and through love, mercy, and compassion, opens a way for us to continue.

SUMMARY

In this chapter we have defined terms that we will be using throughout this book. It will provide the reader with some idea of where we the authors "are coming from," and give us a common language to present and discuss our ideas. We have not chosen "easy" or "popular" definitions for these often controversial terms, but have tried to stick as close as possible to scriptural definitions as we understand them. In general, these definitions should be acceptable to persons from a wide range of Protestant and Catholic Christian backgrounds.

DISCUSSION QUESTIONS

1. How would you define the words "mature years?" In terms of "attitude," "chronological age," or "circumstances" of your life?
2. How do you think about "middle age" and "old age?" Do you look forward to these years as "opportunity" or "liability?" Will you share your reasons for your response?
3. We all have different backgrounds in the "journey" of our religious life. From your experience what does the word "spirituality" mean to you?
4. Have you experienced the gift of the Grace of God in your life? Would you share the experience with the group?

NOTES

1. Tillich, Paul. *Dynamics of Faith.* San Francisco: Harper & Row Publishers, 1957.
2. Fowler, James. *Stages of Faith.* San Francisco: Harper & Row Publishers, 1981.

Chapter 3

Where Are We Now
and Where Are We Going?

Where are we now in our spiritual growth, and where are we going? These are questions that all must answer for themselves, and questions that the faith community must struggle with as a body. Why is this important? Suppose you decided to drive to Los Angeles. What are the steps you will need to take in order to reach your destination? First, you will need to get out a map, locate where you are now, and identify the route you must take in order to reach Los Angeles. Next, you will get into your car and start driving along the route indicated on the map. As you come closer and closer to your destination, you will need information about the place to which you are going so you will know when you get there. Perhaps road signs along the way or the city skyline will give you clues that you are getting closer. In the same way, if you wish to grow spiritually, you will need to know where you are starting from and also something about the place for which you are heading.

WHERE ARE WE NOW?

This section involves asking ourselves some hard questions, and perhaps discussing them with a close friend. This will help us to identify areas of our spiritual life that need working on. Every human being has areas of strength and areas of weakness. The process of "working on" ourselves is lifelong. No one is "there" or "gets there" during this short stay on earth. We only approach it, and most of us are still far away even near the ends of our lives. To progress toward our goals, however, we need to know how far away from them we still are. The apostle Paul encourages us to: "Check up on yourselves. Are you really Christians? Do you pass the test? Do you feel Christ's presence and power more and more within you? Or are you just pretending to be Christians when actually you are not at all?" (2 Corinthians 13:5, LB).

First, are you just pretending? Do you really and truly believe that God exists? This is the fundamental question upon which all else rests. "And without faith it is impossible to please God, because anyone who comes to him *must believe that he exists* and that he rewards those who earnestly seek him" (Hebrews 11:6). If you can give an unqualified "yes" to this question, then ask yourself, "Do I really know this God in whom I believe? Or do I just know *about* God?" "Am I experiencing God on a regular basis in my life?" "Do I consider God in my daily decisions?" "Have I made knowing God the focus of my ultimate concern?"

Be honest with yourself. People have all sorts of ways of fooling themselves in order to avoid the painful realization that they need to change. Changing one's views and attitudes is a difficult process. Most people want to remain exactly where they are and as they are. Aging, however, has a way of thrusting us out of our comfort zones, and into a growth mode. Somebody once remarked how similar aging and gambling were. The longer you play the game, the more likely you are going to lose. Loss or the threat of loss often creates enough pain to motivate people to change. Nothing else motivates like pain does. C.S. Lewis said that pain was God's "bullhorn to a deaf world." How true it is.

Regardless of where you are in your "walk with God," if you are not growing and maturing in this relationship, then you are stagnant or even slipping backward. Because of the energy and effort required for spiritual maturation, there is a natural tendency to allow our faith to drift. However, our relationship with God is like a shark swimming in the ocean. Unless it keeps on swimming, the shark dies. Its very life depends on constant movement forward that allows oxygen in the water to filter through its gills. So will our spiritual life die, unless it keeps growing and expanding. Now ask yourself, "Have I stopped growing spiritually?" "Do I want to grow spiritually?" "Do I need to grow spiritually?" "Am I willing to make the necessary effort required to grow spiritually?" Yes, it will take an effort. Jesus said, "If anyone would come after me, he must deny himself and take up his cross and follow me" (Matthew 16:24; repeated in Mark 8:34 and Luke 9:23). In the great classic *The Imitation of Christ*, Thomas à Kempis writes about our natural reluctance in this regard.

> Jesus has many who love His Kingdom in heaven, but few who bear His Cross. He has many who desire comfort, but few who desire suffering. He finds many to share His feast, but few His fasting. All desire to rejoice with Him, but few are willing to suffer for His sake. Many follow Jesus to the Breaking of Bread, but few to the drinking of the Cup of His Passion. Many admire His miracles, but few follow Him in the humiliation of His Cross. Many love Jesus as long as no hardship touches them. Many praise and bless Him, as long as they are receiving any comfort from Him (. . .). Do they not betray themselves as lovers of self rather than of Christ, when they are always thinking of their own advantage and gain?[1]

WHERE ARE WE GOING?

As maturing Christians, certain characteristics mark our relationship with God and our relationship with those in our family, church, and larger community. In terms of relationship with God, we desire to communicate and interact with our Creator. We want God to be an active participant in our lives. We consult God before making important decisions. We turn to God for comfort when troubles arrive. We celebrate with God our successes and fortunes. When we are uncertain about what course to take, we learn to wait for direction from God. We realize our need to take time to pray, read the holy scriptures, worship and praise God with others. We desire to talk about spiritual matters more than about practical or worldly subjects. We want to give of our time and finances to advance God's kingdom through Christ's church.

We want our relationship with God to come before anything or anybody else in our lives—before family, friends, finances, health, comfort, pleasure, even before our own happiness and personal goals. We do certain things just because we know God wants us to, even when we ourselves would prefer not to. As Thomas à Kempis indicates above, the Christian life is one of obedience, service, and sometimes sacrifice, not just warmth and good feelings. 1 John 5:3 explains plainly what it means to love God: "This is love for God: to obey his commands." Christ said the same thing: "Why do you call me, 'Lord, Lord,' and do not do what I say?" (Luke 6:46). Should we not love God in the way God has asked to be loved?

Next, what characteristics mark our relationships with others in the Christian community and those in the broader community in which we live? Why do we attend church, or go to church-related dinners, potlucks, or bazaars? Is it purely for social reasons to avoid loneliness and make friends? As maturing Christians, we participate in the Christian community in order to share our common love for God with others as we praise, adore, and worship our Creator. We celebrate together what God has done for us and is going to do for us in the future. We listen to, encourage, and help out those who are less fortunate than we are. We experience real pain when we see another Christian brother or sister suffering. We are not only moved to pray for them, but also prompted to go out of our way to help them through their crisis. How can members of a Christian community allow their disabled, infirm, or otherwise suffering brothers and sisters to struggle unaided?

Participation in the Christian community means that each person is following and living the teachings of Jesus Christ. Again we return to what Christ tells us this involves: "By this all men will know that you are my disciples, if you love one another" (John 13:35). Christ himself, then, has made this THE identifying mark by which we are known as his followers–that is, our love for each other. The apostle John writes "If any one says, 'I love God,' and hates his brother, he is a *liar*; for he who does not love his brother whom he has seen, *cannot* love God whom he has not seen. And this commandment we have from him, that he who loves God should love his brother also" (1 John 4:20-21, RSV). Once again, love for God is inextricably linked with love of neighbor. Thus, a complete spiritual life for a Christian community involves each member loving, caring, and serving the needs of each other within the church, as well as serving the known needs of those living in the broader community.

Below is a short list summarizing the characteristics of the Christian life, both in terms of our relationships with God and with others. These are meant as broad guidelines only. They are primarily taken from the two Great Commandments in Matthew 22:36-40 and from Psalm 112. Assuming a healthy love and respect for his or her self, the mature Christian is one who *consistently* makes conscious *decisions* to:

1. seek and spend time with God in prayer, scripture reading, and communal worship.
2. reverence and put his or her complete trust in God in all situations.
3. surrender his or her will to God's will for all of life.
4. care for, love, and serve others, regardless of circumstances.
5. be kind, merciful, and generous to others, regardless of circumstances.
6. be humble, giving credit to the Lord where it is truly due.
7. be thankful for and enjoy the many good things that God brings into his or her life.

A mature spiritual life, then, involves first a deep, consuming love relationship with God; second, a commitment to love and serve the neighbors with whom the Lord has surrounded us–our family first, our church second, and then those in the larger community; and third, a recognition of and appreciation for the many blessings that God grants us daily. Such a life is entirely independent of health or circumstances. These are personal characteristics we seek as Christians. If you do not feel or act in the ways described above, do not be discouraged–you are not alone. Most of us do not feel or act this way even a fraction of the time, and none of us can constantly feel or consistently act as we would choose. God accepts, loves, and appreciates us exactly as we are, but also wants us to continually strive and stretch for our higher calling. It is only by God's grace that we can move forward along this path. Thomas à Kempis puts things in perspective:

> I have never found anyone, however religious and devout, who did not sometimes experience withdrawal of grace, or feel a lessening of devotion. And no Saint has ever lived, however

highly rapt and enlightened, who did not suffer temptation sooner or later.[2]

We all fall far short of achieving mature spirituality, and perhaps we will never fully achieve it in this lifetime. Committing our energy and effort to this goal, however, will place us on the "narrow way that leads to life" (Matthew 7:14). How do we know when we are on the path? Jesus said, "If a man [or woman] remains in me and I in him, he will bear much fruit . . . " (John 15:5). Spiritually maturing Christians are *increasingly* experiencing fruit in their lives–more "love, joy, peace, patience, kindness, goodness, faithfulness, gentleness and self-control" (Galatians 5:22). However, you can judge only yourself in this regard, never others[3] (see the following section, Adversity).

Growth toward spiritual maturity is integrally related to mental health and successful aging. Being filled with God's Spirit, as we saw in Galatians, is accompanied by love, joy, and peace–essential characteristics of good mental health. Despair, depression, anxiety are emotional problems that are epidemic in our society today. This may be due partly to secularization and the removal of God from public as well as from much private life. As people have given up on God, they have been left with huge holes in their lives. These holes they try to fill up with all sorts of substitutes–drugs, alcohol, work, sex, money, seeking of power, as well as a wide range of non-Christian spiritual beliefs and superstitions. This widespread unrest and mental distress is not unexpected, given our society's desertion from the only true way to happiness and wholeness–the path of loving and serving God. This should arouse in us not contempt for the world, but a deep sense of concern and a Divine call to first get our own lives straight and then lead others back to the path of truth.

ADVERSITY: THE GREAT PURIFIER

Circumstances have a way of testing the mettle of our spiritual lives. Seemingly spiritually mature persons whose faith has not been tested by adversity may find their joy and peace quickly vanish when difficult times appear. The opposite is also true. The person suffering great adversity (or vulnerable person[4] suffering lesser adversity) who carries the burden obediently and demonstrates only fleeting joy and peace may indeed be very mature spiritually. Thus, judgments about spiritual maturity cannot be made by external fruits unless all the vulnerabilities and circumstances of the person's life are known—and they are seldom known by anyone but God. A person's spiritual maturity is tested and refined when he or she experiences chronic illness, disability, loss of loved ones, changes in social position, and other losses that become more frequent as we age. Thus, growing older provides tremendous opportunity and motivation for spiritual growth, growth that we need in order to reach spiritual maturity.

TOO OLD TO CHANGE?

You might think, "But I'm too old to change." Well, until recently many would have agreed with you, including Sigmund Freud. Freud claimed that persons over age fifty-five were "unanalyzable," saying that the inelasticity of mental processes in old age prevented any meaningful change. Likewise, numerous mental health experts since Freud's time have emphasized that religious change or conversion occurs primarily in adolescents. Not so say recent Gallup polls, which indicate that among those who experience significant religious change in their lives, only 22 percent experience it during adolescence. While that survey indicated the mean age for such change was twenty-eight years old, it included very few persons over the age of sixty. We did a similar survey of persons age sixty-five or older and found that over 40 percent said that it was not until after age fifty that they experienced a significant change in their religious faith.[5] Many were in their seventies and eighties when this change occurred. Adversity was frequently involved. Thus, it is likely that we are *never* too old to change, *if we want to change.*

SUMMARY

In order to mature emotionally and spiritually, we must first recognize where we are now and learn something about where we are going. We have provided some questions that readers should ask themselves to help them determine where they are in their walk with God. We have also described some characteristics of the maturing Christian and challenged the reader to commit to making the necessary effort and change to strive toward these goals. We point out that adversity is the true test of Christian maturity, and that no one can judge another's level of maturity except God who is all-knowing. Finally, research shows that we never get too old to change and that even persons in their seventies and eighties frequently have life-changing religious experiences.

DISCUSSION QUESTIONS

1. Where are you in your spiritual journey? It could be helpful for each person to draw a symbolic picture of this journey through the years past, and share this with the group. When and what happened? What did it mean at the time? What does it mean now in your Spiritual Life?
2. Is the Lord a very real presence in your life and in the making of decisions, or a goal you are striving to reach?
3. Do you find it more difficult to put your trust in the Lord, whom you cannot see, than in other people or the material things of this world which you can see?
4. What effect may there be on the Christian and his or her witness to Christ, if they feel that they have "arrived" spiritually?
5. Has your faith been tested in difficulties, in times of illness, death of a loved one, change in your social or economic position? Do you feel strengthened in your faith by these times of adversity?
6. Do you set aside time to be with the Lord through prayer, scripture reading, and worship?
7. Can you recall a time when you made a conscious surrender to the Lord?

NOTES

1. Thomas à Kempis. A 1952 translation of the 15th century classic, *The Imitation of Christ*, by Leo Sherley-Price. New York: Penguin Books, 1979, p. 83.

2. Tillich, Paul. *Dynamics of Faith*. San Francisco: Harper & Row Publishers, 1957, p. 80.

3. This refers primarily to Jesus' warning in Matthew 7:1-5. Far too many hidden agendas, even many unrecognized by the judging "evaluators" are caught up in the critiques of others. Nevertheless, we must be discerning. The Bible includes many warnings and admonitions to guard against deceitful leaders and troublemakers (Isaiah 56:10-12; Jeremiah 50:6; Ezekiel 34:1-16; Matthew 5:19-20; 2 Corinthians 11:1-15; 1 Timothy 1:3-7; 4:1-3; 6:3-5; 2 Timothy 4:3-5; Titus 1:10-16; 2 Peter 2:1-22; and many more). False teachers and teachings may unknowingly masquerade as "angels of light" (2 Corinthians 11:15), even some psychological and sociological theories, as well as religious cults.

4. By "vulnerable" we mean genetically and developmentally vulnerable to emotional distress in the face of external trauma or stress. These persons are predisposed to anxiety, depression, or self-absorption because of their hereditary makeup (temperament) or because of traumas experienced during childhood.

5. Koenig, Harold G. *Aging and God.* Binghamton, NY: The Haworth Press, 1994.

Chapter 4

What Is Ahead for Us?

The future for middle-aged and older Americans, from a purely materialistic, worldly view, is not a bright one. Adequate medical and psychiatric care from government-funded programs will likely become more and more difficult to obtain in the next century. This will result from increasing limits on Medicare growth. Already, when only 13 percent of our population is over age sixty-five, reducing Medicare expenditures and other social programs has become a number one priority for policymakers. What will happen when the 74 million baby boomers, born between 1946 and 1965, reach their later years and 25 percent of the United States population is over age sixty-five? People will probably find it hard to get the health services they need, with the poor first being effected and then later, middle-class Americans.

These difficult times, on the other hand, will present a great opportunity for the body of Christ, because it will force us to put our Christian principles into practice. Indeed, this may result in our experiencing for the first time the fruits of peace, happiness, meaning, and purpose in life—those things we have so desperately sought after and which have so cleverly eluded us during times of prosperity. Consider the following societal trends.

CHANGES IN HEALTH

Advances in medicine are extending the lives of those with heart disease, stroke, arthritis, cancer, diabetes, and other physical problems. More and more persons are surviving into late life. Health experts say that a baby girl born today will have an average life expectancy of over ninety years. That is the good news. The bad news is that people are not necessarily surviving to old age living active, productive lives. With advancing age has come chronic illness and disability, problems which modern medicine has improved but is far from eradicating. With our aging population, there will be an increasing number of persons with Alzheimer's disease (from two million currently to upwards of fourteen million in the next thirty years). This is because the most rapidly growing segment of the population are persons age eighty-five or over, almost one-half of whom have symptoms of Alzheimer's disease. It has been projected that the number of dependent older persons requiring assistance will grow in an unprecedented fashion in the early to mid twenty-first century. Along with chronic, disabling health problems come difficulties in adaptation and coping–not only for those with health problems, but also for family members and others who take care of them. Consequently, emotional disorders like depression, anxiety, and alcoholism are likely to become even more widespread than they are today.

ECONOMIC CHANGES

As noted earlier, federal and state resources available to meet the physical and mental health needs of aging Americans are becoming scarcer and scarcer. The Medicare budget increased from 38 billion dollars in 1980 to 140 billion in 1992 to almost 170 billion in 1995. It is worrisome that this rapid budget increase has occurred during a time when the number of older Americans is relatively small. At this rate of growth, there are projections that the Medicare trust fund will be used up between the years 2000 to 2002.[1] Projections also indicate that by the year 2036, baby boomers will have exhausted the Social Security retirement trust fund. Payroll taxes levied on the working population may need to be doubled or tripled to keep the program in operation. Younger people may be unable or unwilling to shoulder this burden. Indeed, younger generations may become more and more open to other solutions to the growing problem of older Americans draining society of its resources (i.e., Dr. Kevorkian's solution).

IMPLICATIONS FOR THE CHURCH

Thus, the future for many middle-aged and older Americans is unlikely to be as secure as it has been for the generation before us. This represents an unusual opportunity for the Church to play a leadership role in ensuring that society maintain respect for older persons in this country (and around the world, since other countries are facing the same dilemma). It also presents a major challenge for religious bodies as they seek to meet the emotional and physical health needs of this burgeoning population. The Church will need to mobilize every possible resource to care for those persons who are unable to obtain government services to meet their mental and physical health needs. And what is the Church's greatest resource? Its members. Christians, then, will need to use their talents and abilities to help their neighbors who will have nowhere else to turn.

And that is good, for it may force us toward a new, deeper level of spiritual maturity. The Christian community has become negligent in its social mission largely because of a lack of necessity. *Necessity,* however, is rapidly approaching (given the state of Medicare and social security). No Christians in the days ahead will be able to bury their talent, say they are too old, not needed, have no purpose, or question why they are still alive. If aging Christians will mobilize unused talents to meet the needs of their less fortunate peers, this may have widespread effect on society–and on younger persons who are in desperate need of role models for their own lives. As they see Christian doctrine lived out in the lives of their parents and grandparents and the "fruit" that results from such behavior, they may be attracted to this lifestyle themselves.

What about retirement? You may think, "I don't want to take on all this responsibility now. I've been working all my life. It's time for me to rest and to let others do the work." This is a normal and expected reaction to what we have been talking about. Retirement, however, is sometimes not all we expected.

RETIREMENT

While most persons look forward to retiring someday, that can be a time of considerable turmoil. This may become more and more true for future generations of retirees, for they are not likely to receive the kind of financial support that previous generations have. Retirement is one of the most defining events in the lifeline of aging. It might be seen as moving into a new and empty house waiting to be furnished. Will it be the familiar and comfortable furnishings from the past? The time clock that disciplined the day and framed the daily routine. The cluttered desk and well-worn chair. The morning greeting. The coffee break shared with others. The satisfied close of the day and locked office door. Probably not. More often, one must take the "golden watch" and "certificate of appreciation" and stand in the doorway of a new and empty house of life.

Entering this new and empty space, there are questions to be asked and answered: "What are my expectations in making this move?" "Was there purpose and planning?" "What of the old can be moved into the new?" As you settle into this new house, you must ask yourself, "What will I do with my time here?" "Do I still have any talents that might be useful to others?" "What resources do I have to expend in this place and share with others?" These questions anticipate the sometimes difficult reality of the dramatic change in meaning, purpose, and lifestyle when a person retires.

Our Western culture is not very empathetic to the circumstances and feelings engendered by this often mandated event. The reality of the experience is frequently betrayed by remarks that picture retirement as "a welcome relief from the routine years of work"; a time for "pleasures and privileges" long awaited; a "reward for long and faithful service." In contrast, retirement often brings feelings of "being over the hill"; "being of little use and value anymore"; and "not capable of production." Retirement can be quite alarming for some. No longer valuable to the workforce, struggling to adjust to a new lifestyle with family and friends, uncertain of a place in the social order, the aging person may experience this time as a lonely, debilitating experience. We suggest that there must be emotional and spiritual preparation for this event, particularly with regard to the *use of time.*

> For everything there is a season, and a time for every matter under heaven: a time to be born, and a time to die; a time to plant and a time to pluck up what is planted; a time to break down and a time to build up. . . . (Ecclesiastes 3:1-3, RSV)

RETIRING FROM GOD'S SERVICE

Does retirement from work and from child-rearing responsibilities also apply to our service to Christ? We recently did a computer word-search for retirement in two versions of the Bible (the International Standard and the American Standard). Nothing came up. Abraham sired Isaac at the age of ninety-nine and was buying property when he was 140 years old. There is no evidence that Moses retired either. He was eighty years old and his brother, Aaron, eighty-three years old, when they went before Pharaoh to ask him to free the Israelites. At 120 years old, Moses was writing songs and active in his leadership role. There is no evidence that Joshua ever retired. He was actively leading the Israelites, writing, and drafting covenants right up to his death at the age of 110 years. Likewise, David ruled as king in Israel for forty years and was an old man when he turned over his throne to Solomon. Both apostles Peter and Paul spent their last days of life in prison, actively communicating with and directing the early Christians from their jail cells. Thus, we conclude from the lives of these great leaders in the Bible that God does not retire people from service. God needs us and wants to use us, regardless of our circumstances, right up to the moment we are called home.

SUMMARY

Because of demographic and economic changes in the United States, life for middle-aged and older Americans in the future is likely to be quite different from what it has been in the past. A need to reduce the costs for health care and government-funded programs is occurring at the same time that increasing numbers of aging baby boomers are requiring more and more services. This will likely result in large numbers of Americans being unable to obtain the mental and physical health services they need. Many of these persons will turn to the church for assistance. Are we as Christians prepared and willing to help meet the needs of our less fortunate neighbors in our congregations and communities? Are we willing to spend our retirement years serving God in this way? We discuss what retirement is like today and how it is likely to change in the future. While all of us will retire from our jobs some day, there is no evidence that God retires us from our Christian service or withdraws the fruits of the spirit that result from such service.

DISCUSSION QUESTIONS

1. What new perspectives have you gained from your own retirement, or from the retirement of another family member or friend?
2. Do you believe the Church is facing a growing challenge to meet the needs of the aging membership? If this is a challenge, in what ways do you see the Christian community responding to meet these needs? What other agencies or organizations of our society are meeting these needs?
3. What role, responsibility, do you see for yourself in the response the Church should make?
4. In your retirement, or that of your spouse, what had been expected or planned over the years?
5. What "gifts" have you discovered about yourself in retirement?

NOTE

1. Associated Press (1993). Medicare trust fund going broke. Fund could be drained by 1998. Durham *Harold-Sun* (April 7, 1993), p. 3.

Chapter 5

What Are Our Needs?

Having considered where we are now, where we are going, and the challenges that lie ahead, let us consider the psychological and spiritual needs of persons in their middle age and later life. Many of these needs fit equally well under psychological or spiritual categories, since these domains frequently overlap. The fulfillment of these needs is vitally related to both psychological well-being and spiritual health. Here, we examine twenty-five needs categorized into those related to self, God, and others (Table 5.1). In Chapter 10 we will explore how serving God helps us meet these needs.

TABLE 5.1. Psychological and Spiritual Needs of Middle Age and Later Life

Needs Related to Self

1. A need for meaning and purpose
2. A need for a sense of usefulness
3. A need for vision
4. A need for hope
5. A need for support in coping with loss and change
6. A need to adapt to increasing dependency
7. A need to transcend difficult circumstances
8. A need for personal dignity
9. A need to express feelings
10. A need to be thankful
11. A need for continuity with the past
12. A need to accept and prepare for death and dying

TABLE 5.1 (continued)

Needs Related to God

13. A need to be certain that God exists
14. A need to believe that God is on our side
15. A need to experience God's presence
16. A need to experience God's unconditional love
17. A need to pray alone, with others, and for others
18. A need to read and be inspired by scripture
19. A need to worship God, individually and corporately
20. A need to love and serve God

Needs Related to Others

21. A need for fellowship with others
22. A need to love and serve others
23. A need to confess and be forgiven
24. A need to forgive others
25. A need to cope with the loss of loved ones

NEEDS RELATED TO SELF

1. *A need for meaning and purpose.* During our earlier years, meaning and purpose came from being a mother or father, provider, nurturer, sustainer of the physical, material, and social needs of life. As one ages and moves into middle and old age, either this purpose has been fulfilled or declining physical abilities prevent us from continuing to receive gratification in these areas. People search for meaning and fulfillment in a variety of ways as they age. Many persons seek fulfillment and meaning in their children, grandchildren, friends, hobbies, and other activities. Most persons seek purpose and meaning from activities which have always given their life value and switch to other sources of fulfillment only with great difficulty. As we age, the sources of meaning and purpose that depend on physical health and vigor are the most vulnerable.

2. *A need for a sense of usefulness.* At any age, people need to feel that they are needed and that what they do makes an impact on someone's life. This need increases as people get older, perhaps because the main developmental task of later life involves *life*

review–a looking back over one's life to determine whether it was all worth it. This includes questions such as:

"Did I meet my earlier goals in the areas of work and love?"

"Did I contribute something positive to society and to the lives of others?"

"Will the lives of my children and grandchildren be better off because of what I did with my life?"

"Did my life make a difference?"

A positive response to this life review results in a sense of integrity and self-esteem, whereas a negative response often ends in despair. It is natural, then, for aging persons to think about whether their lives have been useful or not, and especially whether their lives *continue to be useful.* People need a reason to get up in the morning. If that reason is simply to gratify one's own needs and pleasures, then boredom quickly sets in. People become bored with themselves, and embark on a desperate search for something to relieve them of this awful feeling.

3. *A need for vision.* What are the sources of motivation, excitement, and energy in our lives? More often than not, this involves a goal, a vision, a dream that we want to fulfill. What do you want to accomplish during the precious hours, days, or years left in your life? What do you want to see happen? What is it to which you are looking forward? Many aging persons complain of "feeling tired" a lot. Most of the time, there is no physical reason for this fatigue. It is often because people have no reason to get up in the morning. Every day is the same. They look backward instead of forward ("How good the old days used to be!").

On the other hand, many on their deathbeds have lived months or years longer than their physicians would have expected because they wanted to be around when a grandchild was born, graduated from college, or got married, or some other special event. Vision is not only for the young. If life is to be truly satisfying, regardless of age or circumstance, you must have a *dream.* Your "will to live" depends on this. Scripture says "Where there is no vision, the people perish . . . " (Proverbs 29:18, KJV).

The simplest goal or dream can fuel the will to live, energize your day, and provide a sense of direction and hope.

4. *A need for hope.* Hope–what a glorious thing. Hope means that there are better times and a future to look forward to. Hope means that there will be relief from suffering someday. Hope brings energy to overcome adversity. Indeed, hope is defined by adversity, and loses meaning when there is no struggle or threat. The importance of hope is clearly seen only when it is absent. When hope disappears, the future becomes bleak and meaningless. Life becomes a burden only to be tolerated and endured. Joy vanishes and seems as if it will never return. An anxiety to "get things over with" sets in. A loss of hope is probably the most common reason that people kill themselves. Life simply cannot be endured without hope, without the vision of a future.

5. *A need for support in coping with loss and change.* Loss and change are the defining characteristics of aging. Losses occur in many areas of life: loss of physical vigor, loss of friends and loved ones from death or relocation, loss of social position in family or community, loss of finances, loss of home, even loss of life itself. Not all aging persons experience repeated, traumatic loss. But many do. These persons need to grieve over their losses. Such "grief work" is primarily accomplished by talking about the loss to someone who understands and cares. The need to mentally process a loss is so great that it sometimes propels a person to talk about it to people who do not understand, do not care, and do not want to listen. When persons cannot talk about and mourn their losses, the work of grief is hindered. The simple act of listening, being there and sharing their loss, can provide a grieving person with the opportunity to process his or her situation and move beyond it. Unfortunately, in today's busy world, few people are willing to take the time to listen.

6. *A need to adapt to increasing dependency.* We in the United States are an intensely independent people. Relying on others is seen as a weakness. Above all else, we want to control our own lives and not depend on others. Unfortunately, as a result of improvements in health care that have extended the length of our lives, there often comes chronic illness and disability requiring dependence on others. In 1980, there were approximately two million

severely disabled persons over age sixty-five in the United States. By the year 2040, there will be over twelve million severely disabled older Americans. Most people in this country fear becoming dependent more than anything else—more than physical pain, and often, even more than death itself. Sometimes, however, there is no way to avoid depending on others. If that happens, we need to be able to adjust and adapt to this new lifestyle. Failure to do so results in loss of self-worth and sometimes severe depression. What makes things even more difficult is when those on whom we depend see us as a burden or as a restriction on their lives. This makes adaptation much more difficult.

7. *A need to transcend difficult circumstances.* Persons who are severely disabled and dependent on others (after a stroke or other crippling condition), those who suffer from unrelenting physical pain or other discomforts (arthritis or cancer), or those experiencing some other truly difficult and uncorrectable life situation (caring for an abusive, demented family member, for example), must be able to rise above their situation and find hope and meaning in something else. This is particularly true for those of us with chronic health problems. Physical illness causes strong feelings of emotional isolation. We feel as if no one truly understands what we are going through (and sometimes no one does understand or really cares to). A loving family member, caring friend, devoted physician or other health care professional can help reduce this sense of isolation. What does a person do, however, when family and friends are not readily available, and when health care providers do not have the time or interest to listen?

8. *A need for personal dignity.* As we move into middle age and beyond, new questions arise about our value, about who we are now. Capacities to produce and live without causing hardship on others may be lost as physical illness sets in. As the days of success, popularity, power, and productivity are spent, we must turn to other sources of self-esteem and dignity. If these are not found, then we start feeling bad about themselves, embarrassed, burdensome, and lose our sense of purpose. Depression may develop and the desire to live diminishes. Any solid basis for self-worth and dignity, then, must lie outside of a person's physical capacities.

9. *A need to express feelings.* Feelings are neither good nor bad: they are just feelings. And they need to be expressed and shared with others. This is particularly true for the most powerful of feelings, anger. When bad things happen in life, there is a natural tendency to ask "Why?" often as an expression of rage at God. The anger involved in the question "Why?" however, actually represents a normal and expected stage of grief over a loss. The typical stages of grief are shock and denial, bargaining, anger, acceptance, depression, and resolution. As persons realize that the loss is real and cannot be bargained away, they become angry. The anger is necessary because it protects the person from the full weight of the emotional pain that comes from realizing the extent of their loss. Often the anger is mixed with depression. In order to come to terms with the loss and move to the final stage of resolution, the anger must be given up and the pain experienced and worked through.

10. *A need to be thankful.* There is no greater need, nor greater reward, than the expression of thankfulness. When people are thankful, regardless of how small or large the perceived fortune, there is a release of healthy, positive emotions. Because of the human condition, most people in life get a glass that is about half full. Those with a "positive" attitude are thankful for the half that is full and largely ignore the half that is empty. Those with a negative attitude focus more on the empty half and ignore the full half. We have a selective memory that all too readily brings up failures, misfortunes, tragedies, and old hurts. Quickly we forget about the many gifts and treasures in our lives. Without a sense of thankfulness, our lives will become boring, dreary, and devoid of fulfillment.

11. *A need for continuity with the past.* Most people try to preserve both internal and external structures in their lives. By "internal" structures we mean ways of thinking, reacting, and feeling. By "external" structures we mean our social environment. This need becomes greater and greater as we age. A need to maintain internal and external continuity results from the need to preserve a sense of who we are (self-esteem) and to preserve the relationships with those we love and care about. Different things can interrupt the continuity of our lives, particularly physical ill-

ness and loss of a spouse or other close family member or friend. Sometimes, these events force us to leave our homes and familiar surroundings and relocate closer to adult children. Such a move may disrupt a support network of friends that has taken decades to build up. A move to a nursing home or rest home can do the same thing.

12. *A need to accept and prepare for death and dying.* The prospects of physical illness, death, and dying create anxiety and fear in most people. Illness creates a sense of loss and increased feelings of dependency. As noted before, there is also a sense of isolation, of being alone while having to endure unpleasant treatments, side effects of medication, pain and discomfort from disease. There is also fear about what the illness might mean for the future. These are times when one asks "Who is on my side?" "Who understands what's happening to me?" "To whom may I turn for help, for consolation, for assurance and peace of mind?" What most dying persons fear is not pain, other physical discomforts, or even death itself. Rather, they fear dying alone–dying with no one to stand by them, to watch with them, to comfort and reassure them at the threshold of this new and totally unknown experience. Not only must we get ready for death, we must also plan on how to spend the rest of life that remains.

NEEDS RELATED TO GOD

13. *A need to be certain that God exists.* People need to know the answer to the question, "Does God really and truly exist?" Is someone really out there? Ninety-six percent of the American population say they believe in God or a "higher power." Nevertheless, there often lurks an uncertainty in even the most insistent believer. There is a tiny voice that whispers, "Yes, but what if God does not exist? What if it's all a big hoax? What if this is all you get and then it's over?" People want to be certain of God's existence. Until you have experienced God personally in your life, you can never be sure. Being sure is important.

14. *A need to believe that God is on our side.* Not only do we need to believe that God exists, but also that God is on our side. Maybe God

exists, but what if God is not interested in us? What if God simply created the universe, set it in motion, and then went off to do something else, leaving us humans to fend for ourselves? Or maybe God simply made humans in order to spy on them, catch them in their sins, punish, judge, and condemn them. People need to know that God is for them, loves them, has a plan for them, wants to forgive them, has mercy on them, desires the best and fullest possible life for them. Such knowledge brings peace, hopefulness, confidence.

15. *A need to experience God's presence.* We need to experience God on a personal level. The Creator has made us with a need that only God's presence can fill. When we experience God, we are sometimes filled with a truly incredible, almost indescribable, feeling of awe and wonder. Most of the time, however, God's presence is felt quietly and softly, like a small tug on our hearts. Billy Graham tells the story of a little boy who was flying a kite.[1] It was a beautiful day for kite-flying. The wind was blowing briskly, pushing large billowy clouds across the sky. As the kite went higher and higher into the sky, it became lost in the clouds. A man came along and asked the boy what he was doing. The boy said that he was flying a kite. The man asked him how he was so sure that he was flying a kite, since he couldn't see the kite. The boy replied that even though he could not see the kite, he knew it was there because every once in a while he felt a tug. Dr. Graham advises us not to take anyone's word for God, but rather to experience God for ourselves so that we too can experience God's little tug on our hearts and be sure that the Lord is there.

16. *A need to experience God's unconditional love.* We all need unconditional love. This is not the human type of love that gives wanting something in return. This is the kind of love that loves just because we are. Most of us get this love as a baby. It's the type of love a mother has for her infant. No matter what the baby does—cries in the middle of the night, soils his or her diaper, or knocks over a priceless heirloom—the mother still loves her baby. The baby cannot give anything back in return, yet the mother loves and fusses over her greatest of prizes. Each one of us needs this type of unconditional love, and if we do not get it as an infant and child (and some do not), then we spend our lives searching for it, trying to get it from other people. This search is a hopeless one, however,

because humans (outside of the mother-infant relationship) simply do not love in this way.

17. *A need to pray alone, with others, and for others.* People need a quiet time away from the chaos and busy-ness of the world where they can talk with God and review their lives–a time of deep one-on-one communication with God, when we seek our Savior fervently from the depths of our hearts. The need for such intimate one-on-one communication with God becomes even greater when we experience physical sickness or some other distressing situation. Besides a personal time alone with God, we also have a need to share our common faith and devotion with others. We need the support of others as we call out to God for help and deliverance from a difficult situation. We need to experience the caring physical touch of a Christian brother or sister, as they pray with us and for us over some deep-felt concern. As scripture says, "For where two or three are gathered together in my name, there am I in the midst of them" (Matthew 18:20, ASV). We also have a need to pray for others. As we pray for God's will in their lives, we help to usher in God's plan for them.

18. *A need to read and be inspired by scripture.* God often speaks to us through the Holy Word. Because we need the reassurance and direction that only God can provide, we have a need to read scripture, listen to scripture on tape (or have others read it to us), and hear our pastors expound on it. God makes promises to us in scripture. We need these promises to lift us out of despair and provide comfort, peace, and hope for each day. People need the direction and correction that is found in scripture. Because we are so readily deceived by the things of this world, we need God's guidance so that we will not wander off the path of truth. The lives of great Biblical figures help to reduce our own sense of guilt and hopelessness as we recognize that they too struggled with the same sinful desires and weaknesses with which we struggle. Because they were able to overcome, this gives us hope for our own situations.

19. *A need to worship God, individually and corporately.* Within each of us is a need to worship, worship both privately when we are alone and publicly when we are with others. Humans have demonstrated this need throughout recorded history. If God is not the center of our worship, then something else will take God's place.

Joy, thanksgiving, and awe are released when we worship, when we praise, and when we adore God. Few persons can endure life without some form of worship. God does not need our worship. No, it is we who need to worship and praise—for our *own* emotional, spiritual, and perhaps even physical health and well-being. Consequently, we need a place to worship, a setting that is inspiring and conducive to worship. If we are physically unable to get to such a place, then we need to develop an alternative means of participation by ourselves or with the help of TV or radio.

20. *A need to love and serve God.* We also have a deep need to love, worship, and serve. As we have said before, either God can be the object of our love and service, or other things can take God's place. Frequently, we love and serve material things, money, possessions, jobs, and sometimes other people to the extreme of worshiping them. This is dangerous, for we become servants—either physically or emotionally—to whatever or whomever we dedicate our lives.

NEEDS RELATED TO OTHERS

21. *A need for fellowship with others.* People need people. We need each other. Study after study has shown that people who have a large social network and who feel supported and loved have better physical and mental health than others. Scriptures urge us, "Let us not give up meeting together, as some are in the habit of doing, but let us encourage one another . . . " (Hebrews 10:25). Furthermore, Jesus repeatedly commands us to "love" one another. It is no surprise, then, that most of us continue to need the fellowship of those with whom we have things in common, particularly those who can understand what we are going through. Social isolation, on the other hand, has been shown to predict early death from heart disease and other health problems, as well as suicide.

22. *A need to love and serve others.* Humans possess a basic and healthy need to love and serve each other. When we are not doing this, after a time we become bored, tired, even pessimistic about life and begin feeling worthless and useless. Some persons pos-

sess an unhealthy need to serve others in order to gain the love and appreciation they missed in childhood. When people do not respond as they expect, they become angry and resentful. There are other self-involved people who feel entitled to the love and service of others. If others are unwilling, they try to manipulate and control them. Both of these maladaptive tendencies are unhealthy and destructive both to the individuals and to their relationships.

There are also those who have a natural impulse and ability to lead others. This, too, can be healthy or unhealthy, depending on underlying motivations. Some persons wish to lead because they need to be noticed by others, to be the center of attention. This is called narcissism or self-love. Underneath, these persons usually think very little of themselves and are driven to acquire external praise from others to reassure them that they are important and significant. The healthy impulse to lead is actually derived from a desire to serve. Jesus emphasized this to his disciples James and John when they asked him to put them into positions of leadership and authority over the other disciples (Mark 10:37): ". . . whoever wants to become great among you must be your servant and whoever wants to be first must be slave of all. For even the Son of Man did not come to be served, but to serve and to give his life as a ransom for many" (Mark 10:43-45).

23. *A need to confess and be forgiven.* Guilt is a powerful emotion that can be either good or bad. When it is appropriate to the situation, guilt can help keep us from doing things that would harm ourselves or others. Sociopaths have too little guilt or none at all. They feel nothing when they do things that hurt others. When guilt is excessive, on the other hand, it can lead to anxiety and unhealthy restrictions, as well as interfere with our relationships. Healthy guilt impels us to confess and ask forgiveness from the person we have hurt and do what is needed to make amends. Unresolved guilt can sap us of our energy and joy in life. It is a type of self-punishment directed inward at the self. To be emotionally healthy, we must take the appropriate action necessary to resolve guilt. If after humbly confessing our mistake and seeking forgiveness from the person we have injured, we still experience a sense of guilt, then we may be dealing with the unhealthy kind. The refusal or inability to accept

forgiveness–especially God's forgiveness–makes the resolving of unhealthy guilt very difficult.

24. *A need to forgive others.* Just as we need to be forgiven by others and by God, we also need to forgive others for wrongs committed to us. This need to forgive is so great that failure to do so often leads to mental illness. The distinguished psychiatrist Carl Menninger said that if people were able to forgive each other, then all the mental institutions in the world would soon shut down for lack of business. Unforgiveness leads to resentment and bitterness. These two emotions are enormously destructive to both mental well-being and physical health. Resentment drains a person of joy and peace and destroys relationships. Bitterness is a form of hatred that, while completely sparing its object, eats away at its owner. Research is beginning to link these unhealthy emotions to high blood pressure, heart attacks, and stroke.[2] Forgiveness is the only way to rid oneself of resentment and bitterness. How often should we forgive? "As many as seven times?" asks Peter. Jesus' response was, "I do not say to you seven times, but seventy times seven" (Matthew 18:21-22, RSV). Sometimes you have got to keep forgiving over and over again until the bad feeling toward the other person is gone.

25. *A need to cope with the loss of loved ones.* As persons age, the likelihood that they will lose someone close to them increases. This can be particularly devastating in case of the loss of a spouse or a child. Research has shown that men do much poorer than women after they lose their spouse. One of the reasons for this is that men tend to have a much smaller support network than women do. A man tends to rely more heavily on his wife for emotional support, whereas women tend to have a broader base of support from friends as well as family. The quality of the relationship also has an impact on how well the surviving partner will cope. If the relationship has been a strong, unambiguous one, filled with mutual love and concern, then the surviving partner will do much better (even though grieving the loss may be hard). If, on the other hand, the relationship is characterized by strife, conflict, and unresolved resentments and anger, then the survivor may have a difficult time working through the ambivalent feelings.

MEETING THE NEEDS

Experts have a wide range of opinions on how we can best meet these needs and live a satisfying, fulfilling life. Lining the shelves of bookstores are self-help books on how to find happiness, overcome depression, cope with loss, or otherwise meet psychological and spiritual needs. Much of this expert opinion and popular advice focus on the SELF: "What can I do to meet my needs?" "How can I achieve self-fulfillment?" "How can I improve my self-esteem?" "How can I discover my true self?" We are a society that seeks comfort, happiness, pleasure, and fulfillment as a first priority, while running away from pain, suffering, and self-sacrifice. The Bible has a solution to the human problem that is different from the popular solutions of today. Instead of focusing on self, we are encouraged to focus on God: "Not that we are adequate in ourselves to consider anything as coming from ourselves, *but our adequacy is from God* (2 Corinthians 3:5, ASV)." When we respond to others, meeting their needs and sharing their trials, we offer ourselves to God in much the same way that Christ offered himself for us on the Cross.

We believe that the popular strategy of focusing on self is misdirected. In our estimation, the Biblical solution is simply more effective. Systematic scientific research is finding that persons who have a strong religious faith and spend time supporting and caring for others, not only experience greater well-being, higher life satisfaction, and less emotional distress, but also are healthier and may even live longer.[3]

SUMMARY

In this chapter, we described a number of important psychological and spiritual needs of middle-aged and older adults. We also suggested briefly how we can most effectively meet these needs, something that we will more fully elaborate in Chapter 10. We reject the contemporary solution of focusing on the self in order to achieve fulfillment. Instead, we propose that our deepest psychological and spiritual needs are met when we come to love God more than anything else in our lives, and then serve God by serving others with the unique and special gifts the Lord has given us. The next chapter deals with the first step: getting to know and love God with our whole heart, mind, and soul.

DISCUSSION QUESTIONS

1. Record on paper the needs you have in each of the three categories: Self, God, and Others. Would you share these with the group?
2. Do you feel that your life has made a difference in society, in your family? Are you familiar with the process of *Life Review?* This involves looking back on and recording the events, gifts, difficulties from your current and past family life, social life, and working life. Have you done this recently?
3. What is your personal "vision" for your future? Is it a vision fueled by hope, purpose, and meaning, or is it a vacuum of purposelessness?
4. Do you see God as a loving, caring Person with a plan for your life, or do see God as a distant disciplinarian?
5. Has scripture been a source of strength and comfort for you and a form of communication between you and God?
6. Is it difficult for you to accept forgiveness from God or from your neighbors? Is it difficult for you to forgive and put the hurt in the past?

NOTES

1. Brown, Joan W. *Day by Day with Billy Graham*. Minneapolis, MN: World Wide Publications, 1976.

2. Williams, Redford. *Anger Kills*. New York: Random House, 1983, or *Trusting Heart*. New York: Random House, 1989.

3. Hays, Judith C., Landerman, Lawrence R., George, Linda K., Flint, Elizabeth P., Koenig, Harold G., and Blazer, Dan G. *Social Risk to Mood States in Late Life*. Durham, NC: Duke University Medical Center. In preparation.

Koenig, Harold G. *Is Religion Good for Your Health? The Effects of Religion on Physical and Mental Health*. Binghamton, NY: The Haworth Press, 1997.

Koenig, Harold G. *Research on Religion and Aging*. Westport, CT: Greenwood Press, 1995.

Krause, Neal. Chronic financial strain, social support, and depressive symptoms among older adults. *Psychology and Aging*, vol. 2, pp. 185-192, 1987.

Krause, Neal, Herzog, A. Regula, Baker, Elizabeth. Providing support to others and well-being in later life. *Journal of Gerontology*, vol. 47, pp. P300-P311, 1992.

Chapter 6

Knowing and Loving God

A Pharisee asked Jesus, testing him, "Teacher, which is the greatest *commandment* in the Law?"

Jesus replied, " 'Love the Lord your God with all your heart and with all your soul and with all your mind.' This is the first and greatest commandment."

–Matthew 22:35-38

Everything–*everything*–begins with our personal relationship to God. This may seem simplistic and obvious to many of us, and hardly worth repeating. For many of us, however, this relationship is not the central motivating force for our lives. We do many things for reasons other than our love and devotion to God. We stress this relationship here, however, because it is the very engine, the source of power and strength, that enables us to move toward our spiritual and emotional goals. Without it, we soon become discouraged and overwhelmed, unable to sustain the necessary effort during the difficult times which we are certain to face. Charles Allen said "Before a person can live rightly with one another, serve one another, love one another, he or she must first get right with God."[1] Thus, the very first step in the process of renewing your spiritual life is coming to God for confession, for release and healing, and for strength to change.

Our first step is to be sure there really is a God. Many educated persons and experts stress that the modern man or woman should remain open and questioning in things with regard to religious matters. This is true to the extent that we should not limit our ideas about what God can do. Nevertheless, God's existence should not be a debatable question. According to Psalm 14:1, only "The fool says in his heart, 'There is no God.'" Likewise, the book of Hebrews reinforces "And without faith it is impossible to please God, because anyone who comes to him must believe that he exists and that he rewards those who earnestly seek him" (Hebrews 11:6). Perhaps the only way we can be sure that something exists is if we actually experience that something. I am certain that I have a daughter because I know her and have experienced her existence. I am certain that she exists. How might we come to know God in the same way that I know my daughter? We must first know something about God. *Knowing about God,* however, is not sufficient. We must also come to *know God* based on some type of firsthand experience.

KNOWING ABOUT GOD

Before we can get to know someone, we must know something about the person. Does he or she want to be known or loved by me? Will he or she love me back? This also applies to knowing God. What is our Creator like? Does God want to be approached and known by us? Will God love us back? We learn about God in two primary ways. First, the holy scriptures tell us much about what God is like, especially as revealed in the person of Jesus Christ. Second, we learn about God through the example and teachings of other persons.

Knowledge About God from Scripture

We believe that the Bible was written by human beings who were inspired by God. It is a dependable source of information that has guided millions of people for hundreds of years. The scriptures presented in Table 6.1 provide us with a detailed and vivid description of God. While the Old Testament gives a wealth of information about God, it is the New Testament that gives Christians the clearest picture of God in the person of Jesus Christ, who is the "exact representation of his [God's] being" (Hebrews 1:3). In summary, what is God like?

TABLE 6.1. Descriptions of God in the Bible

Old Testament

All-powerful (Genesis 35:11, 43:14, 48:3, 49:25)
All-knowing (Isaiah 48:3-5; Psalm 147:5)
Ever-present (Psalm 139:7-12; Proverbs 15:3)
Unchanging (Numbers 23:19; Psalm 102:27; Malachi 3:6)
Deeply caring (Genesis 50:24; Leviticus 26:12)
Loving (Deuteronomy 7:8-9; Isaiah 43:1-7, 49:14-16; Jeremiah 31:3; Psalms 36:5-8; and others)
Concerned (Exodus 4:31)
Gracious (Isaiah 30:18)
Patient (Exodus 34:6)
Forgiving (Numbers 14:18)
Compassionate (Psalm 103:13; Isaiah 63:9)
Dependable and trustworthy (Isaiah 49:15)
Protecting (2 Chronicles 16:9; Ezra 8:22-23, Psalms 27:4-5, 34:7, 46:1-3, 125:2; Proverbs 18:10)
Healing (Exodus 15:26)
Jealous (Exodus 34:14; Deuteronomy 4:24, 5:9, 6:15)
Judging (Psalm 96:10,13)
Punishing sin (Exodus 34:7; Numbers 14:18)

New Testament **(descriptions of Christ)**

All-powerful (Matthew 28:18; Luke 1:37; Philippians 3:20-21)
All-knowing (John 16:30; Colossians 2:3; Hebrews 4:13; 1 John 3:20)
Ever-present (Acts 17:27-28)
Creator (Colossians 1:16-17)
Unchanging (Hebrews 1:12; James 1:17)
Holy (Luke 1:35)
Sinless (2 Corinthians 5:21)
Protecting (Luke 21:8; Romans 8:35-39)
Gentle (Matthew 11:29)
Patient (Romans 2:4, 3:25; 2 Peter 3:8-9)
Generous (Luke 15:11-31)
Compassionate (Luke 6:35-36, 7:13; Mark 1:41, 8:2-3; Hebrews 4:15; and over 70 others)
Merciful (Hebrews 2:17)
Loving (Matthew 5:43-48; John 3:16; Romans 5:8; 1 John 3:1)
Forgiving (Luke 23:34)
Righteous Judge (Matthew 25:32; John 5:22; Acts 17:31; Romans 2:16; 2 Timothy 4:1)

God is all-knowing, ever-present, all-powerful, the creator and sustainer.

God is loving, caring, compassionate, merciful, and kind.

God is generous, accepting, and forgiving.

God is consistent and dependable.

God is fair, just, and aware of all the facts, the only one who can truly judge us.

These scriptures describe a God with *personal characteristics.* Our God has emotions–anger, love, hate, compassion, mercy–and longs for a relationship with people. In many ways, God is like us. But the Creator is also a lot more than us, and perhaps is more than we can ever imagine. Scriptures indicate, though, that God is enough like us to allow for a personal, intimate relationship: "So God created man in his own image, in the image of God he created him; male and female he created them" (Genesis 1:27). In fact, the Lord is the only one who can really and truly understand us. God knows everything we have been through and all our attitudes and hopes and dreams. God desires to relate to us, to be deeply involved in every one of our hopes, joys, pains, losses, and fears. God responds to each of us, personally and individually. In the movie *Oh, God,* which stars George Burns, there is a scene where God is gambling with the Devil. Here, in order to save one person's soul, God puts everything on the line. God is like the shepherd who leaves his or her flock to look for the one sheep that is lost (Matthew 18:12) or like the father who generously and without question accepts back the prodigal son. Yes, God is extraordinarily committed to us ("spiritual Israel"). The Lord tells us so in no uncertain terms:

> Can a mother forget the baby at her breast and have no compassion on the child she has borne. *Though she may forget, I will not forget you!* (Isaiah 49:15)

> Though the mountains be shaken and the hills be removed, yet my unfailing love for you will not be shaken nor my covenant of peace be removed. (Isaiah 54:10)

> I will betroth you to me forever; I will betroth you in righteousness and justice, in love and compassion. (Hosea 2:19)

For I am convinced that neither death nor life, neither angels nor demons, neither the present nor the future, nor any powers, neither height nor depth, nor anything else in all creation, will be able to separate us from the love of God that is in Christ Jesus our Lord. (Romans 8:38-39)

Knowledge About God from Others

We can also come to know about God by the example and teachings of mature Christians. This is most often our minister, pastor, or priest, but it can also be another responsible, mature person whose life is under the lordship of Jesus Christ. Such persons should have a strong and consistent devotional life of prayer and meditation, a loving concern for others, and a disciplined and exemplary lifestyle. Humility, kindness, sensitivity, and compassion are essential traits. Finally, it is difficult to really love and reach out to others unless the person is mentally healthy and spiritually alive. While it is very important to be open to the teachings and advice of others, we must always remember that God calls every person to be discerning and responsible for what he or she takes in. Seeking guidance and counsel is one thing, abdicating responsibility and blindly depending on someone (other than God) for direction is quite another.

KNOWING GOD

Let all our employment be to *know* God; the more one knows Him, the more one desires to know Him.[2]

As we have said before, knowing about God is different from *knowing God*. We come to know God through firsthand experiences with God. While such experiences are difficult if not impossible to create, plan, or force, there are certain settings and situations that enhance our ability to come into contact with God. First, not only can we learn about God from scripture, but we can also experience God there. Second, we can experience God during periods of devout prayer, meditation, worship, singing, or receiving of the sacraments. Third, we can experience God in the beauty and wonder of creation—a lovely sunset, a still lake, the roar of the ocean, the blowing of the wind. Fourth, we can experience God during periods of suffering and trial (as Job did).

Experiencing God in Scripture and Preaching

The Lord speaks directly to us in scripture, either when we read it ourselves or when we listen to it being preached from the pulpit. We can hear God speak, though, only if we are believing, seeking, expecting, and listening–getting on God's wavelength. When we are on God's wavelength, the biblical passages come alive with meaning and significance (". . . his sheep follow him because they *know his voice*"–John 10:4). God also speaks to us through the words of mature and gifted Christians as they read the holy scriptures and preach about them. As we listen with open, attentive, and discerning minds, we allow God to communicate his love, wisdom, and direction to us.

Experiencing God in Prayer and Worship

We can also experience God during times of sincere, devout prayer or meditation. This can occur when we are praying alone, or when we are praying with others. When we are alone, we can talk with God at any time of the day or night. Effective prayer includes time to both speak and listen.

When Jesus was asked by his disciples how they should pray, he gave clear and explicit instructions (Luke 11:2-4, KJV). He said, "Our Father which art in heaven, Hallowed be thy name." Recognizing who God is and who you are, come to God with an attitude of humility and adoration. "Thy kingdom come. Thy will be done, as in heaven, so in earth." Recognize that God has a plan and a desire for you and all of mankind. Try to get your will in line with God's will so that you will desire what the Lord desires. "Give us day by day our daily bread." Having recognized who God is, humbled yourself, and resolved to align your will with God's will, then you may petition for the things you need in your life. "And forgive us our sins; for we also forgive everyone that is indebted to us." God reminds us that we must admit that we have sinned, repent for those sins and forgive others, before the Lord will answer our prayers. "And lead us not into temptation; but deliver us from evil." We conclude by asking

God for protection for our lives so that we will not be tempted to sin again, but will have the strength to make every right decision.

The steps to effective prayer, then, are: (1) recognizing who God is and that God is present; (2) recognizing who you are and humbling yourself; (3) aligning your will with God's will, seeking those things that God would want for you; (4) repenting for sins of pride and willfulness and forgiving others for sinning against you; and (5) recognizing that you cannot do it alone and need God's help and protection. You are now in a position to talk with and hear from God. Faith, sincerity, and humility are keys that open the doorway of communication.

We can also experience God when worshiping with others. Like prayer, worship begins with praising God, i.e., recognizing and paying tribute to who God is and that God *is*. Scripture says, "O thou that inhabitest the praises of Israel" (Psalm 22:3, KJV). God promises to be right there when we worship and praise together. Expressing recognition and thanksgiving for all that the Lord has done, both in the past and the present, can help move us closer still to God. Music can powerfully facilitate this process. Through music, we can express praise, adoration, and thanksgiving to God, mobilizing our emotions so that we can feel God's presence and deep love for us.

In the same way, we can experience God as we participate in holy communion and confess our sins. As we receive communion, we remember the great redemptive sacrifice that Christ made for us. We come into the presence of Christ as we receive the blessed bread and wine offered as symbols of his body and blood offered up as a sacrifice for us; it reminds us that both our physical and spiritual lives come from and are sustained by God. As we confess our sins, we humble ourselves and admit that we are powerless to control our lives and ask for God's forgiveness and strength. Through these acts, we take on an attitude where we are able to hear and experience God in forgiveness.

Beauty of Creation

"For since the creation of the world God's invisible qualities–his eternal power and divine nature–have been clearly seen, being understood from what has been made . . . " (Romans 1:20). The wonders of nature give us a sense of awe and suggest a greater power behind it all, as we gaze at a beautiful sunset, the opening of a flower, the wide expanse of stars on a clear night, the peace of a quiet pool in the forest, or the view from a high mountain top. We also sense our finiteness and helplessness when we are in the midst of a raging storm, watch the waves of the ocean pound on the beach, or fly in an airplane. In many ways, nature communicates to us that all of this around us is not here by chance, but by the grand and intelligent design of One who is greater and higher than us. Even more awesome than creation is the fact that the Creator loves, cares about, and wants to relate to each one of us.

Suffering and Pain

Our Creator, Redeemer, Savior is alive today and wants to be involved in our lives. Sometimes, though, it takes the bullhorn of pain to force us to let God in. When things are going great and there is no anxiety, unrest, or pain in our lives, we seldom experience the energy or motivation to "draw near to God." Charles Allen quotes Psalm 23 in this regard,

> Sometimes God puts us on our backs in order to give us a chance to look up: "He *maketh me* lie down." (Psalm 23). Many times we are forced, not by God, but by circumstances of one sort or another to lie down. That can be a blessed experience. Even the bed of an invalid can be a blessing if he takes advantage of it![3]

Suffering is an emotional response to loss. Losses come in many forms, some more obvious, others less obvious. The more obvious losses are loss of health; loss of loved ones through death or relocation; or loss of possessions. The less obvious losses involve loss of love from others (rejection); loss of social, work, or family position; loss of youth and productivity; loss of freedom to do as one chooses; loss of the ability to deny that someday we will die; or loss of expectation of meeting goals, hopes, or dreams. Loss creates an uncomfortable feeling inside us that will not go away. This is where the energy lies that may push us out of ourselves and closer to God, or for some of us, further away from God and deeper into ourselves.

The Book of Job reports on the life of a man who encountered tremendous suffering and loss. His physical illness ("sore boils from the sole of his foot unto his crown") and suffering (loss of his loved ones, family, and possessions) were not a consequence of sin or because of wrong decisions on his part. As the King James Bible says, "There was a man in the land of Uz, whose name was Job; and *that man was perfect* and upright, and one that feared God, and eschewed evil" (Job 1:1, KJV). How do you get better than "perfect"? Like most persons in Job's situation, Job questioned why the Lord was allowing this to happen to him and pleaded to be allowed to die, rather than go on suffering. God answered Job in the midst of his suffering by giving him an experience of the Lord's presence. It was by his suffering that Job was humbled to the point that he was capable of experiencing God. It was at that point that Job's calling was renewed. From then on, he lived a full and prosperous life. We will also have an opportunity to meet God during our most intense times of suffering and painful loss. Look and search for God there.

COMING INTO GOD'S PRESENCE

Knowing God requires a personal and individual experience of God's presence in our lives. According to theologian James Fowler, this is where "conventional" faith leaves off (believing for the sake of one's family or community), and "individuative reflective" faith begins (believing because one is deeply convinced that it is true). To be deeply convinced of God's reality and presence, we need an experience of that presence that goes beyond simple head knowledge. How did the great men and women of faith in the Bible come to experience God? By humbling themselves, confessing the error of their ways, and then committing or recommitting their lives back to God. In the Old Testament, this was often accompanied by a sacrifice of something dear to them to symbolize their devotion to God, sincerity of commitment, and atonement for sin.

In Genesis 22, Abraham built an altar to sacrifice his son Isaac to God, demonstrating his faith. In Exodus 30, the Lord commanded Moses to build an altar for burning incense that would be placed in front of the Ark that contained the Ten Commandments, and said to him "I will meet with you there" (Exodus 30:6, LB). In Judges 6,

Gideon tore down his father's altar to Baal and built an altar to God that symbolized a new beginning and a challenge to the old, evil ways of his time. In 2 Samuel 24, David built an altar to sacrifice to God in order to atone for his sin of pride and stop a plague that was killing many Israelites; this was an altar of confession and seeking forgiveness to hold back God's judgment.

In 2 Chronicles 4, Solomon built an altar for sacrifices as part of completing the temple. The Ark of the Covenant was brought into the Inner Sanctuary, the most holy place underneath the wings of the Cherubim; this symbolized God's new dwelling place among his people. After the Israelites had been defeated, the temple destroyed, and many carried off to Babylon, the king of Persia allowed some Israelites to return to Jerusalem to rebuild the temple. When they returned, they rebuilt the altar of God as their first action and made sacrifices on it to worship and thank the Lord (Ezra 3); this was an altar of new beginning and revival. Finally, in Isaiah 6, Isaiah had a vision of God's glory and power, had his lips touched with a burning coal from the altar to take away his guilt and atone for his sins, and was called to become a messenger of God. This place where Isaiah experienced God was an altar of purification where he was anointed for his calling.

As you can see, altars were places signifying new beginnings where people came into God's presence, were purified and forgiven and, often, received or reaffirmed their calling. While the Israelites made sacrifices at these altars, it wasn't the sacrifices themselves that God wanted. It was something beyond sacrifice that really delighted the Lord. What was it? David gives us a clue in Psalm 51.

> You do not delight in sacrifice, or I would bring it; you do not take pleasure in burnt offerings. The sacrifices of God are a broken spirit; a broken and contrite heart, O God, you will not despise. (Psalm 51:16-17)

This "broken" spirit and heart refer to a person humbling him or herself to God, confessing faults and wrong decisions, and opening oneself up to God. It is in humility that we take our eyes off ourselves and become capable of experiencing and communicating with God. Otherwise, our sins of pride, self-concern, and worldly preoccupation blind us to God, who is always present and capable of being experienced.

Before the priests in the Old Testament could go into the holy of holies to meet with God at the main altar (Exodus 27), they had to cleanse themselves on the altar of incense outside the veil of the temple that separated the outer court from the inner holy of holies (Exodus 30). It was at this altar that they were made clean and pure enough to go into God's presence in the holy of holies. When Jesus Christ died on the cross, the veil in the temple tore from top to bottom (Matthew 27:51). We are no longer required to cleanse ourselves at an altar before coming into God's presence (Hebrews 6:19-20, 9:26). His death and resurrection is our sacrifice, if we accept it, to make us clean enough to meet with God. Christ is alive now, making intercession for us (Hebrews 7:25). With faith in Christ, then, we are freed to approach God directly. Our faith is weak though, and our sins of pride, self-concern, and worldly preoccupation so great that it may seem impossible for us to come into God's presence.

A small book entitled *Closer than a Brother* (Winter, 1971, Shaw Publishers) is a reinterpretation of the great classic "Practicing the Presence of God" written by Brother Lawrence in the mid-seventeenth century. Brother Lawrence was a simple man able to experience and stay in God's presence throughout the day–when alone, with friends, and even when at work in his soup kitchen. The fruit that his life bore proved that this was an unusual person experiencing something very real and important to both spiritual and mental health. He was a kind, gentle, loving man who always had time for others, and who frequently experienced deep and profound joy in life. When asked about his relationship with God, he emphasized the importance of understanding what "grace" really means:

> We want to earn God's approval . . . but even the best we can do would fall far short of that. God gives it to us, in the middle of our failures–if we put our trust in him, and love him, and give him first place . . . And that's the key . . . I've learned that all he really wants is me . . . and living all the time as though he were there. And he is. He's really there . . . not just 'in heaven,' but right here in the cafeteria . . . . If I've got him, what else could I possibly need? (pp. 29-30)

As Brother Lawrence says, there is nothing we can do to earn God's approval. The Lord gives it to us freely. There is nothing for which we can claim credit. This is not self-denigration or false guilt. Our human nature makes us extraordinarily self-centered and eager to meet only our needs. *The realization of God's tremendous gift to us as sinners—the right to come into the Lord's presence and experience the Creator—creates in us an attitude of appreciation, thankfulness, and openness that allows us to see and experience God.*

Thus, in order to enter into God's presence, it takes faith (a belief that God exists), humility (facing who we really are), confession (admitting our faults and asking for forgiveness), and surrender (turning control of our lives to God, making the Lord and doing the Lord's will the focus of our ultimate concern). The apostle Paul summarizes our task as follows: "Therefore, I urge you, brothers, in view of God's mercy, to offer your bodies as living sacrifices, holy and pleasing to God—this is your spiritual act of worship. Do not conform any longer to the pattern of this world, but be transformed by the *renewing of your mind*" (Romans 12:1-2). It is a free gift, but in another sense, it requires your whole life.

When asked about how he first entered into God's presence, Brother Lawrence responded as follows:

> I set out first, to think through his divine existence—that he really and truly and objectively exists, as Someone quite other and apart from me, his creature. That was first, and I thought of him and all I knew of him from the Scriptures and in my experience until I was total convinced that *God is*. I had no intention of spending my life in the presence of a Being who was simply a figment of my imagination. Then I spent hours letting that tremendous truth impress itself deeply on my heart—my feelings, if you like. Slowly, by letting my mind lead my heart, and by letting the light of faith shine into my feelings, I came to a point where my faith was alive and growing. I had absorbed, first, the knowledge, and then the love of God, and I resolved to do all I could to live from then on in a continual sense of his presence and, if possible, never to forget him again. There was no studied reasoning to prove the existence of God,

and no elaborate meditation to inflame my devotion to him. But I had been in his presence—the living God—and I never wished to leave it ever again.[4]

Brother Lawrence had a deep and special relationship with God. This was not the result of a single experience, but rather due to his spending time with God. Likewise, Martin Luther said,"I cannot afford not to spend time with God."

SPENDING TIME WITH GOD

At least six things happen when we spend quality time alone with God. *First*, a friendship develops with God as you come to know the Lord, experience the Lord's care and love for you, and realize that God alone in this world is *really and truly for you*. This friendship will displace your sense of loneliness and isolation in this world and make you less dependent on others to meet your every emotional need. When asked what he considered to be the best way of coming closer to God, Brother Lawrence (p. 62) said:

> . . . do my ordinary, everyday business without any view of pleasing men, but as far as I can, purely for the love of God. That was what St. Paul was talking about . . . "Am I now seeking the favor of men, or of God? Or am I trying to please men? If I were still pleasing men, I should *not be a servant of Christ.*" (Galatians 1:10, ASV)

Second, you get strength from God to handle trials and difficulties in life: ". . . greater is he that is in you, than he that is in the world" (1 John 4:4, KJV). In order to be used as God's instrument in this world, you will need plenty of strength. Loving and serving others often requires great patience and perseverance. You simply cannot love others in an unconditional way without God's grace and strength. In fact, it is only from the strength gained through your relationship with God that you can love others in this way (see Chapter 9).

A *third* consequence of spending time with God is that you will develop God's character. Character building is never pleasant. You will feel more guilt when you sin and a greater need to make amends.

You will be naturally drawn away from sin, and toward truth, mercy, compassion. According to Brother Lawrence,

> But my experience is that when we are faithful to keep ourselves in his presence, and keep him constantly "before our eyes," it keeps us from willfully offending him, and so preventing his grace and power from flowing into our lives. (p. 68)

You will also begin to hate evil and injustice. The prophet Habakkuk was infuriated by what was going on in the world of his day. "Why do you make me look at injustice? Why do you tolerate wrong? Destruction and violence are before me; there is strife, and conflict abounds. Therefore the law is paralyzed, and justice never prevails. The wicked hem in the righteous, so that justice is perverted" (Habakkuk 1:3-4). Along with an increasing intolerance for injustice, however, you will feel more and more love for the sinner who is entrapped by evil, and perhaps even feel pity and sorrow for the person, as Jesus did (Luke 19:41-42).

A *fourth* result of spending time with God is that you will develop a hedge of protection about your life. This does not mean that bad things will not happen, for God "sends rain on the righteous and the unrighteous" (Matthew 5:45). According to Billy Graham,

> Nowhere does the Bible teach that Christians are to be exempt from the tribulations and natural disasters that come upon the world. It does teach that the Christian can face tribulation, crisis, calamity, and personal suffering with a supernatural power that is not available to the person outside Christ.[5]

Your perception of events around you will not cause as much anxiety, fear, or loss of hope. This is because your well-being is no longer tied to your circumstances or to the events that happen in your life. Your real treasures are in heaven "where they will never lose their value, and are safe from thieves" (Matthew 6:20, LB). A person will become emotionally attached to whatever he or she invests time and money in. Being primarily attached to God helps to protect us emotionally from the distress caused by changing circumstances in our lives.

A *fifth* result of spending time with God is that you will learn to hear God's voice as the Lord speaks quietly and gently to you in the many situations of your life. Jesus said, "The man who enters by the gate is the shepherd of his sheep. The watchman opens the gate for him, and the sheep listen to his voice. He calls his own sheep by name and leads them out. When he has brought out all his own, he goes on ahead of them, and his sheep follow him because they know his voice" (John 10:2-4). You will not be able to hear or distinguish God's voice from the loud clatter of the world or from your own thoughts unless you learn to recognize the Lord's voice. Knowing God's voice not only enables you to hear your divine calling, but also to live out that calling with the assurance the Good Shepherd is caring for you. When ministering to others, ongoing communication with God is absolutely essential in order to be sensitive to the person's real needs and know how to meet those needs.

A *sixth* consequence of your spending time with God is that you will receive *vision*–God's divine perspective on your calling in life. This vision is the driving force, the motivating force that will enable you to continue ministering to others, even when the going gets rough and your natural drives give out. "Where there is no vision, the people perish . . . " (Proverbs 29:18, KJV). Without a vision or Divine calling, you will tend to wander. You will be distracted by other things that are more exciting and less difficult but yield only brief, temporary, or shallow pleasure. People without vision often ask questions such as "What can I do to stop feeling bored?"; "What can I do with my time?"; "What can I do to give me pleasure?" and so forth. In contrast, those who are pursuing their vision or calling in life have little time to ask such questions, as they are focused on fulfilling their goals.

SUMMARY

Our relationship with God must be our greatest concern, for this is the source of the power necessary to push us along the path toward our spiritual and emotional goals. We develop a relationship with God by (1) being sure that God exists, (2) learning more about God, and (3) knowing God by experiencing God in our lives. Our belief that God exists starts out on faith. As we learn more about God and personally experience God in our lives, God's reality becomes more and more certain to us. We *learn about God* by reading the holy scriptures and by listening to the teachings and observing the life examples of mature Christians. We come to *know God* as God speaks to us in the holy scriptures and through others, and as we experience God in devout prayer and worship, the beauty of creation, and the pain of suffering. God's grace and our humility makes this possible. As we spend time with God, certain things begin to happen: we develop a close friendship with God; we receive strength to handle trials and difficulties; we develop Christ's character; we receive a hedge of protection about our lives; we learn to hear God's voice; and we receive God's vision and calling on our lives.

DISCUSSION QUESTIONS

1. When and how did you first become aware of God's existence in your life?
2. What does it mean to you to say "Jesus Christ is Lord"? How do you witness to this in your life?
3. Share some of the attitudes and actions of fellow Christians which have been "faith" building in your life.
4. Scripture describes God as longing to have a relationship with us. What means does God provide for us to respond to this longing?
5. Is it difficult for you to accept the fact that we cannot earn God's approval by our "good works" but only through the Lord's free gift of Grace?
6. Six things are listed that can happen to us when we spend quality time alone with God. Have you experienced any or all of these six consequences?

NOTES

1. Allen, Charles L. *God's Psychiatry.* Grand Rapids, MI: Fleming H. Revell, 1953, p. 46.
2. Brother Lawrence. The practice of the presence of God (17th Century). In *The Treasury of Christian Classics*, Westwood, NJ: Barbour and Co, p. 52 (no date).
3. Allen, Charles. *God's Psychiatry.* Grand Rapids, MI: Fleming H. Revell (Baker Book House), 1953, pp. 18-19.
4. Taken from Brother Lawrence's *Practicing the Presence of God* as retold by David Winter in *Christian Classics in Modern English.* Used by permission of Harold Shaw Publishers, Wheaton, IL 60189.
5. Tillich, Paul. *Dynamics of Faith.* San Francisco: Harper & Row Publishers, 1957.

Chapter 7

Our Call to Serve

Who is the Almighty, that we should serve him? What would we gain by praying to him?

—Job 21:15

And now, Israel, what doth the Lord thy God *require* of thee, but to fear the Lord thy God, to walk in all his ways, and to love him, and *to serve the Lord thy God with all thy heart and with all thy soul,* To keep the commandments of the Lord, and his statutes, which I command thee this day *for thy good.*

—Deuteronomy 10:12, KJV

God needs each and every one of us to participate in the Creator's plan for humanity. We are the Lord's hands to touch and reach out to others; we are the Lord's arms to hold and comfort others; we are the Lord's mouthpiece to encourage others; we are the Lord's legs and feet to walk next to and lead others. God has chosen not to do this without us, because the Lord knows that we as humans spiritually, psychologically, and perhaps physically, need to serve our Creator in this manner. Age and physical status do not disqualify us from this calling. As we noted in Chapter 4, this is a lifetime commitment from which there is no retirement. Sickness, disability, total incapacitation, and dependency are not sufficient reasons to retire. Nobody retires from God's service. As long as we are conscious and possess even the most rudimentary ability to know and think, we can continue to serve and receive the spiritual and psychological benefits of such service.

As noted before, modern psychology and many Christian books talk about the importance of "being," as opposed to "performing." We agree that if a person's worth in life depended on performance and productivity, then this attitude can be dangerous for someone who is aging and may someday lose their ability to perform. Nevertheless, we believe this applies to "performing" when the reason for doing things is to get others to appreciate or value us. It does not necessarily apply to performance in the sense of serving God who provides opportunities for us to serve in every situation. Remember that in our computer search of the Bible, we could not find anything about people retiring from God's service or any persistent emphasis on the need to simply "be" and forgo action, *particularly when action is possible and possibly required.*

The book of 1 John underscores the importance of action, of loving and serving God through loving others. In fact, John makes this the primary criterion for "knowing" that we know God.

> We know that we have come to know him if we *obey his commands*. The man who says, "I know him," but does not do what he commands is a liar, and the truth is not in him. But if anyone obeys his word, God's love is truly made complete in him. (1 John, 2:3-5)

> Everyone who loves has been born of God and knows God. *Whoever does not love does not know God,* because God is love. (1 John 4:7,8)

How do we know that we love God?

> No one has ever seen God; but *if we love one another,* God lives in us and his love is made complete in us. (1 John 4:12)

> Anyone who does not do what is right is not a child of God; nor is anyone who does not love his brother. (1 John 3:10)

> If anyone says, "I love God," yet hates his brother, he is a liar. For anyone who does not love his brother, whom he has seen, cannot love God, whom he has not seen. And he has given us this command: *Whoever loves God must also love his brother.* (1 John 4:20-21)

> This is how we know what love is: Jesus Christ laid down his life for us. And we ought to *lay down our lives for our brothers.* If anyone has material possessions and sees his brother in need

but has no pity on him, how can the love of God be in him?
Dear children, let us not love with words or tongue but *with
actions* and in truth. (1 John 3:16-18)

Thus, the Bible *commands* us to love others, and to love them "with
actions and truth."

RESPONDING TO GOD

Serving God requires seeking (spending time with the Lord and
being open to instruction), careful listening, obedience, and action.

I will show you what he is like who *comes to me* and *hears my
words* and *puts them into practice.* He is like a man building a
house, who dug down deep and laid the foundation on rock.
When a flood came, the torrent struck that house but could not
shake it, because it was well built. (Luke 6:47-48)

In today's society, which cherishes independence and self-direc-
tion, obedience is an unpopular term that turns people off. Obedience means doing something that you are naturally inclined not to
do, particularly in response to the request or command of another.
God often asks us to do things that we do not want to do, that we do
not think we have the talent to do, or that we do not feel prepared
to do. If you are spending regular time in God's presence, you will
hear a voice quietly but consistently urging you to do things that
you may not want to do. Obedience means doing them with the
trust and faith that if God is calling you to do something, then God
will provide everything you need to be successful.

The Christian life is one of responding to God's directions. "This
is love for God: to obey his commands" (1 John 5:3). The way we
show our love for God is by doing what God asks us to do. This is
an essential feature of making Christ the Lord of our lives: "Why
do you call me, 'Lord, Lord,' and do not do what I say?" (Luke
6:46). Jesus says that we will be rewarded for such obedience both
now and afterwards:

What good will it be for a man if he gains the whole world, yet
forfeits his soul? Or what can a man give in exchange for his

soul? For the Son of man is going to come in his Father's glory with his angels, and then he will reward each person according to *what he has done.* (Matthew 16:26-27)

Rather than stay in your house and watch an entertaining TV program, for example, God may be urging you to call a lonely person in your church or go to visit and bring him or her a meal. You may not feel like spending time with this person, or you may not feel that you have the ability to cook a meal for this person, or a dozen other excuses may arise to block your path. If you step out in faith, however, you will be rewarded. Such actions are likely to have completely unpredictable benefits on your behalf. Thus, obedience brings rewards from sources that only God could orchestrate, and as you experience all this, your faith will grow stronger and stronger.

SERVING OTHERS

Loving and serving others was the distinctive mark of those who followed Christ (John 13:35). When asked in Luke 10:25-27 by a Jewish lawyer (expert in the law) what a person must do to inherit eternal life, Jesus turned the question back and asked him what was written in the law. The lawyer's response was that one must not only love God, but must also "love your neighbor as yourself." Jesus' response was "You have answered correctly. Do this and you will live." Thus, according to Jesus, you cannot inherit eternal life unless you love your neighbor as well.

This requirement is a difficult one for many. We often come across people in our lives who are unpleasant, rejecting, hateful, cunning, manipulative, deceitful. Indeed, it may seem unreasonable to require that we, self-centered and self-preoccupied as we are, be as concerned about others as we are about ourselves. Could this have been a mistake on Jesus' part? Or maybe it was just one of those things that found its way into the Bible and, like women being required to cover their heads in church, is one that we can now simply ignore. Probably not. In that scripture, Jesus was asking a Jewish expert in the law to quote what was written in the Old Testament. God had made the point clear to Moses in Leviticus 19:18-19 where the Lord said:

Do not seek revenge or bear a grudge against one of your people, but *love your neighbor as yourself. I am the Lord. Keep my decrees.*

Not only is Jesus' directive to love our neighbor contained in Luke and Leviticus, but it is repeated at least five other times in the New Testament (Matthew 22:39, Mark 12:31, Romans 13:9, Galatians 5:14, and James 2:8). The apostle John goes so far as to say, "For anyone who does not love his brother, whom he has seen, cannot love God, whom he has not seen" (1 John 4:20). He is saying that you cannot and are not obeying either of the two Great Commandments, if you do not love your neighbor.

The key to getting out of this predicament is perhaps one's interpretation of the term "neighbor." Obviously this means the people I know and love—my friends, family, buddies at church, and so forth. Even loving my friends and family in this manner, you might think, seems a formidable task. But Jesus does not stop there. He goes on to explain what he means by the term "neighbor," blocking all possible routes of escape. Basically, Jesus says that "neighbor" means *anyone needing your help.* Even people who believe differently from you, even people you do not know personally, even people you do not particularly like, even your *enemies.* If any of these people need your help (like the crime victim helped by the Samaritan on the road to Jericho), you are required as a follower of Christ to help them (Luke 10:30-37). This means we have got our work cut out for us. There is plenty for all of us to do, given a world full of needy neighbors, millions on this continent and billions on others. And if we decide "No, I don't want to associate with such people," or "Somebody else will take care of that need," or "I don't have the time to help out," then Jesus has already prepared a response for us (Matthew 25:41-45).

Gallup surveys indicate that over half of the American population indicate that religion is very important in their lives, and over two-thirds of older Americans make this claim. What is not clear, however, is what people mean when they say that religion is important in their lives. The apostle James defines religion as the action of visiting and caring for those who are lonely, helpless, or suffering.

> Pure religion and undefiled before God and the Father is this, to visit the fatherless and widows in their affliction, and to keep himself unspotted from the world. (James 1:27, KJV)

If you have really captured what we are saying, then you may be feeling a bit disturbed now, just as King Josiah felt when, after his priest discovered the Book of the Law, he realized that they were not following the laws contained in it ("When the king heard the words of the Law, he tore his robes" [2 Chronicles 34:19]). It is hard for us as authors to write this, because we know that we ourselves have not been as faithful in loving our neighbor or as responsive to those in need as God has asked us to be. It may be particularly difficult for those of you who are not feeling well, are in pain, or are suffering in some other way, to fulfill this commandment. But sickness or suffering cannot excuse us. Indeed, there are no excuses that anyone can give or should give. In whatever situation we find ourselves, we are required to love our neighbor. Period.

We clearly cannot do this on our own, as God anticipated. That is why Christ told us first and foremost to focus on the greatest commandment which was to develop a relationship with God. It is through the gift of the Holy Spirit that we receive the strength, inspiration, and motivation to love each other. It was Jesus' promise that he would not leave us without such a gift. As he promised to his disciples just before his final ascent into heaven, so he promises to us, "But you will receive power when the Holy Spirit comes on you; and you will be my witnesses in Jerusalem, and in all Judea and Samaria, and to the ends of the earth" (Acts 1:8). We are Christ's witnesses when we love and serve others for his sake.

While loving others unconditionally may seem an impossible task to some, we must persist in our efforts and, with the apostle Paul, "press on toward the goal to win the prize for which God has called [us] . . . " (Philippians 3:14). God knows and understands each of our circumstances. Even a small effort to love others by someone who is experiencing sickness, depression, or some other difficult situation in life, will be recognized by God and rewarded, just like the widow who placed her two mites into the offering basket was praised by Jesus because she gave all she had (Mark 12:41-44).

COUNTING THE COST

> If anyone would come after me, he must deny himself and take up his cross and follow me. (Mark 8:34)

Yes, serving God is not always easy. For this reason, Jesus warns us to "count the cost" (Luke 14:28). When we minister to those who are suffering from pain or depression, it is easy to feel weighed down by the problems that person is experiencing. This type of suffering should be expected. It is part of bearing the other person's burden and is a necessary part of the ministry we have chosen. Just as Christ was persecuted, we too will be persecuted. *The persecution you will experience can take many subtle forms, but whatever form it takes, its intention is to stop you from performing the service you have been called to do.* Just as Christ decided freely to take up his cross, you must freely decide to take up your cross and follow your Lord–and following often involves suffering and difficulty. You need to be prepared for it and willing to endure it. That is the cost.

This type of suffering, however, is not like the suffering that you might have experienced in the past when it was forced upon you and not of your own choosing. You will discover that there is a certain joy in your heart that accompanies suffering that is "chosen" and willingly endured for right intentions. "For just as the sufferings of Christ flow over into our lives, so also through Christ our comfort overflows" (2 Corinthians 1:5). The early Christians had many trials and troubles, and many even got depressed. However, they counted their suffering for Christ not as a burden to run away from, but rather as an honor that Christ had chosen them to suffer and witness for him in what was then and is today a mighty spiritual battle for the freedom of the world. Billy Graham says it this way:

> They never forgot what Christ Himself had gone through for their salvation; and to suffer for His name's sake was regarded as a gift rather than a cross. Christians can rejoice in tribulation because they have eternity's values in view. When the pressures are on, they look beyond their present predicaments to the glories of heaven. The thought of the future life with its prerogatives and joys helps to make the trials of the present seem light and transient.[1]

Even if you are suffering over something that you did not choose, that you do not want (like sickness, pain, disability, loss of loved ones), you may still decide whether you are going to fight against the suffering or willingly bear it. For the Christian, no suffering need be pointless (Romans 8:28), although sometimes we need to search pretty hard or wait for a long time to find the point. According to Brother Lawrence (p. 56),

> We've got such a limited perspective–a sort of "worms's-eye view" of life. It might look quite different from God's viewpoint.

When experiencing a difficult life situation that cannot be changed by any effort on our part, and we willingly decide to accept the suffering and be a witness for Christ in that suffering, then we will transform our "unwanted" suffering into an "accepted" suffering, enduring it in the same way and for the same reasons that the early Christians did. There is, of course, a *tremendous psychological and spiritual advantage* for bearing a suffering willingly for this purpose. As we stop struggling against our burden, and perhaps blaming God or others for it, the burden immediately becomes lighter (as Christ promised us in Matthew 11:28-30). There are a number of reasons why this occurs.

First, there is emotional distress involved in carrying around something you do not want. Much energy is expended over frustrating thoughts such as "I don't deserve this," "Why did this happen to me?" "Look at everybody else without this problem," "I don't want to live my life like this," and so on. Second, the most burdensome aspect of suffering is feeling it has no meaning. When you accept your suffering willingly for Christ, you endow it with *meaning and purpose*. Every ache, every pain can be used (by your attitude) to advance God's kingdom on earth. Third, you will begin to share in some of the joy and sense of honor experienced by the early Christians as they participated in Christ's suffering and witnessed for him to the world. Fourth, people will probably like being around you more and will wonder how you are able to handle things so well; this will provide you with an opportunity to share Christ with people and experience the joy that accompanies such activity.

The apostle Peter addresses the issue of accepted suffering, emphasizing that those who choose to serve Christ will invariably encounter hardships and trials, but they should persist anyway because they will be rewarded for their faithfulness:

> Dear friends, do not be surprised at the painful trial you are suffering, as though something strange were happening to you. But rejoice that you participate in the sufferings of Christ, so that you may be overjoyed when his glory is revealed . . . if you suffer as a Christian, do not be ashamed, but praise God that you bear that name . . . So then, those who suffer according to God's will should commit themselves to their faithful Creator and continue to do good . . . And the God of all grace, who called you to his eternal glory in Christ, after you have suffered a little while, will himself restore you and make you strong, firm and steadfast. (1 Peter 4:12-19; 5:10)

Although Peter is primarily referring to painful trials that result from being persecuted because of one's belief in Christ, this also can apply to persons who are suffering for other reasons. By deciding to accept our suffering and bear it for Christ's sake, we become like the early Christians who suffered because of their love for Christ. In either case, it is *love for Christ* that motivates the acceptance of suffering and the positive attitude that results (see also 2 Corinthians 12:1-10).

Thus, choosing to love and serve God with our lives has a cost; it will involve some degree of pain and suffering on our part. Compared with the burden of loneliness, boredom, and a useless life, however, it is a light load (Matthew 11:28-30). We need to trust God that this is true, because the Lord has promised this in the Bible and has vowed to never leave or forsake us nor to lead us astray (Hebrews 13:5).

REWARDS FOR SERVICE

The scriptures are filled with promises to and rewards for those who respond to God's call to love and serve those in need. Here are just a few.

> Blessed is he who has regard for the weak; the Lord delivers him in times of trouble. The Lord will protect him and preserve his life; he will bless him in the land and not surrender him to

the desire of his foes. The Lord will sustain him on his sickbed and restore him from his bed of illness. (Psalm 41:1-3)

So if you faithfully obey the commands I am giving you today—to love the Lord your God and to serve him with all your heart and with all your soul—then I will send rain on your land in its season, both autumn and spring rains, so that you may gather in your grain, new wine and oil. I will provide grass in the fields for your cattle, and you will eat and be satisfied. (Deuteronomy 11:13-15)

And ye shall serve the Lord your God, and he shall bless thy bread, and thy water; and I will take sickness away from the midst of thee. (Exodus 23:25, KJV)

If you keep my commandments, you will abide in my love just as I have kept my Father's commandments and abide in his love. These things have I spoken unto you, *that my joy be in you, and that your joy may be full.* (John 15:10-11)

These scriptures emphasize that if we love and serve God by serving others, not only will we experience greater joy and satisfaction in life, but God will protect us in our own time of need or sickness. This was certainly the case for John Wesley, founder of the Methodist Church, who actively served God preaching and teaching right up to his death at the age of 88. In 1788, at the age of 85, Wesley wrote:

I am not so agile as I was in time past (. . .).
I have daily some pain (. . .).
I find likewise some decay in memory with regard to names
  and things lately passed.
My remnant of days I spend in his praise.
Who died the whole world to redeem:
But be they many or few,
My days are his due,
And they all are devoted to God.

YOU CANNOT DO EVERYTHING

Remember that no one person, not even one church congregation or parish, can do everything. How does one choose among the dozens or hundreds of human needs and the possible ways to meet them when we are so finite in time, energy, resources, and competing obligations of work, home, church, and community services, each of which deserve attention? We must learn to establish priorities. As we will learn in the chapters ahead, each of us possesses a special talent or gift that enables us to serve in a particular manner. These gifts and talents that God gives us are meant to complement each other, each slightly different from the others and all needing all the others. It is the body of Christ working together than enables us to meet the vast human need that surrounds us.

> Just as each of us has one body with many members, and these members do not all have the same function, so in Christ we who are many form one body, and each member belongs to all the others. We have different gifts, according to the grace given us. (Romans 12:4-6)

SUMMARY

In this chapter we examined scriptures that explain what love of God really means, i.e., that we respond to God's call to love and serve others. God needs each and every one of us, regardless of our health or particular circumstances, to participate in God's great plan for humanity. It may sometimes be difficult to serve God in this way, and we should therefore, "count the cost" of such service. While our salvation is not dependent on it, the joy and happiness that we experience in this life may indeed be. God assures us that the burden of serving in this way is much lighter than the load that the world would have us carry, and that this "chosen" suffering will be accompanied by rewards that will surprise and delight us in ways that only God can orchestrate. None of us can meet all the needs of those around us, but if each of us will commit to using our special gift or talent to serve in a particular area, then together as the body of Christ we can meet the need.

DISCUSSION QUESTIONS

1. Have you heard a call from God to serve in a particular way? Have you stepped out in faith and obeyed this call?

2. What risks might you have taken in your community for the cause of serving Jesus Christ?
3. Has it occurred to you that while offering your services to neighbors in need, you are serving the Lord as well and obeying his commandments?
4. Why is it possible to meet difficult circumstances and even suffer with joy and thanksgiving?
5. Has it been your experience that in serving others you have found deeper satisfaction in life, greater joy, and an increasing devotion to God? Please share some examples?

NOTE

1. Thomas à Kempis. *The Imitation of Christ*, translated by Leo Sherley-Price. New York: Penguin Books, 1979.

Chapter 8

Identifying Our Talents

Now there are varieties of gifts, but the same Spirit; and there are varieties of service, but the same Lord; and there are varieties of working, but it is the same God who inspires them all in everyone. To each is given the manifestations of the Spirit for the common good.

–I Corinthians 12:4-7

Every good gift and every perfect gift is from above, and cometh down from the Father of lights . . .

–James 1:17

DISCOVERING OUR GIFTS

In Chapters 6 and 7, we examined (1) our need to know God, (2) our need to love and serve our neighbor, and (3) God's promises of reward for this service. In this chapter, we ask you to turn inward and examine yourself in an effort to discover the unique gift or talent that God has given you. We believe that using your talent to bring happiness, comfort, and hope to others will help you achieve spiritual maturity, emotional health, and satisfaction in life. Someone once said that it is not possible for us to find happiness for ourselves by searching for it. We were created in such a way that only by providing happiness to others can we find it ourselves. To neglect or bury your talent, ignore the needs of others, and make the search for happiness and fulfillment in material pleasures and comforts your main goal in life, will almost guarantee a shallow life (Matthew 6:33). Charles Allen gets right to the point when he says,

> Each of us is an investment. Our responsibilities differ in that to some have been given five talents, others two, and to others one. But to take what we have received, be it little or much, and to fail to increase it, is to become a "wicked and slothful servant" . . . Jesus did not find it necessary to warn us against becoming gangsters and murderers, but very clearly does He condemn those who pass by on the other side of a wounded brother. The very foundation of this commandment is the fact that God values every man as He values me.[1]

The search for your talent begins by thinking about (1) what you enjoy doing, (2) what you have skill in, and (3) how that can be used to benefit others—members of your family, church, community, or others with whom you have frequent contact. This may be a skill that you used earlier in your life on your job. Or perhaps it is a service that you provided your children when they were growing up. Or maybe it's an old hobby. For some, this talent may be quite obvious. For example, a retired carpenter or electrician might use the skills of their trades to create modifications in the homes of disabled, homebound people to make their lives easier. Other less obvious skills may require careful thought and, perhaps, discussion with others.

You may say, "Well, I don't have any special skill or ability that would be useful to others." We would disagree, because we believe that every person, at every age, in every circumstance, has a unique talent, ability, or gift, which at least partly explains why he or she is in that situation. Table 8.1 provides examples of gifts or talents that God has given us. We have subdivided them into emotional, spiritual, instrumental, and rarely recognized gifts. Your particular gift has been fashioned for the special circumstances that you are now in. Many of these gifts and talents can be used not only in person, but also over the telephone, by letters, e-mail, and other ways. The discovery of your talent and its use in serving God by serving others will help make your life meaningful and purposeful. Ultimately, it will lead to the fulfillment of the deepest needs outlined in Chapter 5.

TABLE 8.1. Examples of God-Given Gifts, Talents, and Abilities

Emotional Gifts

Listening — The ability to sit quietly, focus attention on, and actively listen to another person

Understanding — The ability to understand and feel the pain that another person is going through in a situation

Kindness — The ability to display acceptance, warmth, and concern toward another person

Appreciation — The ability to thank others, to recognize and honor the work that they have done (however small, insignificant, or even inadequate)

Praise — The ability to praise others for things they have done, to build them up (must be sincere, not false flattery)

Encouragement — The ability to support, foster, help others to complete a goal or task that is difficult for them or help them endure a stressful life situation

Companionship — The ability to be a companion to someone, accompany them places, relieve their loneliness and isolation

Counsel — The ability to give wise advice and direction for another person's life

Endurance — The ability to withstand physical or emotional pain, yet keep a positive attitude and friendly demeanor

Humor — The ability to bring humor or laughter to an otherwise difficult situation

Smiling — The ability to smile at others in a warm and sincere manner, conveying a sense of friendliness and welcome

Spiritual Gifts

Prayer — The ability to pray in a deep and sincere way for the special needs of others (both in private and with others)

Spiritual counsel — The ability to discern God's will in a situation and communicate that gently and effectively to others

Preaching — The ability to communicate spiritual truths to others and inspire them to implement them in their lives

TABLE 8.1 (continued)

Instrumental Gifts

Helping	— The ability to provide practical assistance in a chore, either helping someone else accomplish something or doing something for yourself that would lighten the load of others, including those caring for you
Cleaning	— The ability to clean, sweep, vacuum, or dust for a person who is too disabled to do these tasks, or who needs help because of caregiving or other responsibilities
Respite Caretaking	— The time to sit with a physically or mentally ill person, or baby-sit small children to give their regular caretakers an opportunity for refreshment or for performing some other ministry
Transportation	— The ability to provide transportation for others to places they need to go, e.g., church, doctor's office, shopping, visit family, volunteer work, other ministry
Electrical	— The ability to identify and fix problems with electrical systems, fixtures, wiring, etc.
Plumbing	— The ability to identify and fix problems related to water or sewage pipes and appliances
Carpentry	— The ability to build and fix things, like modifying a disabled person's house so that they can use the bathroom or move about more easily
Mechanical	— The ability to repair and service cars or machines
Repairman	— The ability to fix things in general
Painting	— The ability and equipment to paint the inside or outside of houses, etc.
Gardening	— The knowledge and the ability to grow plants and landscape
Computer skills	— The ability to work with computers, and to teach others about them
Cooking	— The ability to prepare food and meals for others, and to serve them
Cosmetics/Hair	— The ability to help others with their appearance, cut hair, etc.
Reading	— The ability to read a book or magazine to someone who is blind or cannot read
Writing	— The ability to write, put yours or others' thoughts in writing, including poetry

Interpreting	— The ability to help one person communicate with another, either by translating a foreign language, doing sign language for a deaf person, or otherwise acting as an intermediary in a situation between people where they are not able to communicate
Medical	— The knowledge and ability to identify and help manage people's health problems or provide them with information and referrals about these problems
Teaching	— The ability to communicate information, educate or train others in a skill or about an area of knowledge
Nursing	— The knowledge and ability to identify and care for the needs of those with health problems or disability (take blood pressure, give medication, or teach about health issues)
Accounting	— The possession of knowledge and ability to help with economic or financial problems, taxes, bills, Medicare, social security
Business	— The knowledge and ability to do business wisely with others
Sales	— The ability to sell things, to convince others about an idea
Organizational	— The ability to organize and accomplish tasks so that things are done correctly and efficiently
Administrative	— The ability to get persons to work together toward a common goal
Legal skills	— The knowledge and ability to handle legal issues, power of attorney, guardianship, wills, suits
Philanthropy	— The ability to provide money to buy things for other persons that they need to help make them more self-sufficient or fill some other dire need or to contribute to ministries
Music	— The ability to play an instrument, sing, or conduct
Drama	— The ability to act or to direct plays or other productions
Art	— The ability to paint, make pottery, or create something else (photos, sculpture, carving, and so forth) that inspires others
Craft-making	— The ability to make something with your hands that might be useful to others (sewing or crocheting, toy-making, etc.)

TABLE 8.1 (continued)

Rarely Recognized Gifts

Health	— Being physically and mentally healthy, capable of meeting your own and others' needs
Disability	— Being in a state where you are physically disabled and dependent on others for your needs. You have the ability to permit others to minister to you, providing them with the opportunity to serve God by meeting your needs
Poor hearing	— Being unable to hear well. You have the ability to provide others with the opportunity to serve God by being considerate of you (speaking in a voice that you can hear and understand) and patient with you (repeating what they say when at first you do not hear it)
Poor vision	— Being unable to see well. You have the ability to provide others with the opportunity to serve God by looking for you, reading to you, and assisting you to get about.
Depression	— Being sad or discouraged about a situation. You have the ability to provide others with an opportunity to serve God by seeking to encourage and comfort you, taking time to listen to you and understand you*

---

*This is your gift if you have done everything in your power to overcome the depression. It is not to be used to solicit sympathy from others. In fact, depression is your gift only if you do not want other people to bother you or minister to you; if you feel that way, then you will be ministering to them by allowing them to minister to you.

EXAMPLES OF DIFFERENT GIFTS

Let's take an extreme case to show that every one of us, regardless of circumstances, has a talent that he or she can use to serve God. This is a real case about a woman who suffered a stroke that resulted in a tragic neurological condition called a "locked in" syndrome. Jane, as we will call her, was an active, vibrant woman in her eighties before the stroke, which suddenly left her completely paralyzed. All the muscles of her body and face were affected. Only her eyelids were spared. Nevertheless, she remained alert and completely aware of her surroundings. Jane was placed on a respirator and had to be fed by a plastic tube surgically placed through her abdominal wall into her stomach to keep her alive. Her urine was drained off into a bag that hung from her bed. She had no control over her bowels, and stool slowly oozed out of her rectum. She had to be diapered, cleaned, and turned every couple hours. She was completely helpless and dependent on others. The only way she could communicate with the outside world was by blinking her eyelids. The nursing staff taught her a code using her eyelids. Two blinks meant "yes," three blinks meant "no," and so forth. Jane could do absolutely nothing to help herself. To her, this was a meaningless, useless life. All she could do was wait until death would end her agony. Understandably, she was very depressed.

One day, Jane's pastor came by for a visit. As usual, he read from the scriptures and spoke comforting words. But he was under a great deal of stress himself that day. He had a heavy administrative load and things were not going well financially at the church. Many in his congregation were elderly and sick, had family difficulties, or were struggling with some other type of life problem. The pastor began talking about some of these stresses, including how guilty he felt because he had no time to pray for those in his church who were going through tough times. Jane had always been a devoutly religious woman. She had coordinated a prayer chain in the church prior to her stroke. Suddenly, an idea came to the pastor. He asked Jane if she would be willing to pray on a regular basis for him as well as for the persons in the congregation who were having problems. She blinked twice indicating "yes," and her face appeared to brighten a bit.

The next day, he brought in a list of persons and situations that needed praying for. The list was suspended from the top of Jane's bed so that she could read it. When the pastor returned a week later, he found Jane with a bright look in her eyes–quite different from the dull, dazed, and hopeless look a week ago. Members of the congregation began to visit Jane to tell her about the amazing things that were happening in each of the situations that she had been assigned to pray for. Jane eventually caught pneumonia and died, but those around her reported that her spirits increased tremendously once she found that she could do something that might be useful to someone else.

As long as we are conscious and have the ability to think and reason, we can always be used by God to serve others and help to bring about God's kingdom on earth. We challenge anyone who claims that sincere, heartfelt prayer is of no use, or that even the most disabled and dependent person is not capable of praying for his or her caretakers, nurses and doctors, family members, or persons in their church or wider community.

Some amazing scientific research has demonstrated the benefits of prayer. One study showed that prayed-for patients hospitalized in a coronary care unit of a large metropolitan hospital actually did much better (required fewer medications, antibiotics, respirator assistance) than patients who were not prayed for. The remarkable thing about this study was that patients did not even know they were being prayed for, and those who prayed for them, did not know the patients personally and were many miles distant from them.[2] If people *know* they are being prayed for by loved ones who *know whom they are praying for*, the effects of prayer are likely to be even greater. Thus, we all have the unique and powerful gift of prayer that we can use whenever we wish to benefit those around us.

Norma, another real patient, recognizes that she has a special gift that she can serve God with. She has never been married, lives alone, and is a simple person with little education or training. Norma has a number of medical problems including diabetes, problems with her stomach, and difficulty moving about because of a mild stroke. Nevertheless, she does not let these health problems keep her down. Norma is actively involved in her church, attending both Sunday morning and Sunday evening services. Although unable to drive because of visual problems, she catches a ride with friends who live nearby. She remains active in her church and has taken on the responsibility of calling members of the congregation who are not at church on Sunday to be sure that they are OK and that there is nothing they need. She also keeps track of who is in the hospital and who has lost loved ones, and writes get-well or sympathy cards to encourage them. She buys the cards at the local grocery store at $2.88 for a box of twelve. She always includes her telephone number in the card. Norma is using her gift of "time" to love and serve others.

Sarah suffers from severe degenerative arthritis. She lives in a nursing home, where she receives total care from the nursing staff. Though mentally alert, she must be helped with toileting, bathing, even getting in and out of bed into a chair. Her roommate, Peggy, has a similar condition with about the same level of disability and care requirements. Peggy has become negative and complains constantly about the care that she receives. She is frequently pushing her call light, requesting help for different things from the staff, and bitterly talks about them behind their backs because they do not respond immediately to her demands.

Sarah, on the other hand, is determined not to feel useless or be an excessive burden on others. Like Jane and Norma in earlier cases, Sarah has a strong relationship with God. She decides that she will serve God by serving those around her in any and every way she can. When the nurses come in to care for her, she greets them with a friendly smile and asks how their day is going. She makes every effort to help herself and make as little work as possible for the nursing staff. Whenever they finish working with her, she thanks them and tells them how much she appreciates their hard work. She frequently asks them if there is anything she can do to help out around the home, and they give her small responsibilities that she can perform. Sarah also takes an interest in the lives of the nursing staff, and for this reason they often open up to her about the problems they are experiencing and sometimes even ask her advice. In her free time, Sarah knits things for the nurses and for her roommate, Peggy, and prays for them and their individual needs. In this way, Sarah uses the talents she has (a smile, a friendly and appreciative attitude, the ability to pray, and the use of her arms and hands) to give her life meaning and improve the lives of those around her. Her quality of life is better than many of her friends who are still healthy and completely independent.

Six months ago, Ruth's husband of forty-five years died following a five-year battle with cancer. She was a devout Christian and actively involved in her church. After her husband's death, however, she withdrew from her friends and church family. After a time of intense prayer and seeking God's will for her life, Ruth realized that her special gift in life was *the insight she gained from suffering* over the death of her husband. She started back to church again, despite her own grief, and began to talk with another woman in the church whose husband had also recently died. Ruth shared how she missed her husband terribly at night, but found that reading the Psalms and other Biblical passages comforted her. Ruth discovered that talking with the other woman seemed to help both her own pain and the pain of the woman. This inspired Ruth to start a Bible-based bereavement group in her church. About ten recently widowed women were soon attending the group that met once a week. Ruth then opened the group up to women in the local community. Before long the group expanded so much that it had to be broken into subgroups that met at different churches. Ruth endured something she would have never voluntarily taken on herself (the death of her husband). Through this experience, however, she learned something that she was able to use to benefit others. She used this gift, her own insight gained through suffering, to help build up other widowed persons in her own church and then later, others in the community.

William's case is another one that shows how we can use our talents, even when they appear small and insignificant. William suffered a stroke about one month ago which left him unable to walk, confined to a wheelchair, and unable to speak. He had a clear mind, though, and the use of his hands. In his earlier days, William had prided himself in being handy with a pocketknife and had done quite a bit of whittling. After the stroke, however, William stopped everything. Day after day he sat in his wheelchair staring blankly out the window of his room. Then one day, William's pastor came by for a visit. The pastor asked him how he was getting along. William, unable to speak clearly, wrote on his communication board "lousy." He followed with "What reason do I have for being here? Why doesn't God just take me? I'm of no use to anybody anymore." The pastor had known William for many years. In fact, they had gone to the same high school together. He remembered that William had always been good with a knife and wood. He asked William if he had done any whittling lately. William wrote down "Haven't thought about it." The pastor suggested he try it again so he'd have something to do with his time. The pastor also mentioned that the church was involved in a ministry to a nearby orphanage and that the children there were badly in need of toys.

William took the pastor up on the suggestion and began whittling again. The pastor arranged for a member of his church to bring William the sticks of wood he needed. After several months, William began producing small wooden whistles, cars, even airplanes for the kids at the orphanage. After several months, the pastor drove him over to the orphanage to meet the children. To his surprise, he had become famous around there because of his wooden toys. A number of the children began writing to him. Although William lived only another two years after that, he never again felt useless or worthless.

EVERY LIFE HAS A PURPOSE

What about people who are demented or even unconscious? How can their lives have meaning or purpose? We are such an action-oriented society that we do not value being the recipient of care, nor do we value those who require such care (we think of ourselves in the same way that we think about others). Demented or uncommunicative persons may be participating in God's plan by giving others an opportunity to provide love and concern for them. Take, for instance, an elderly grandmother with advanced Alzheimer's disease. The grandmother's daughter may require that her children visit their grandmother in the nursing home and bring little presents to show their love and appreciation. Over the months or years of such visits, the grandchildren are learning something. This will help them become less self-centered and more focused on the needs of others as a result of caring for their grandmother. Thus, the grandmother is playing a vital role in the emotional and spiritual growth of her grandchildren. We must recognize the valuable contribution that every person (regardless of physical or mental state) can make to God's great plan for humanity.

TALENTS DO CHANGE

Our talent or gift can change with time as our circumstances change. Take for example the talents of Jim, an electrician, and Sally, a schoolteacher. At age forty-five, Jim used his skills as an electrician to help inspect and fix electrical problems in the homes of elderly people who couldn't afford to pay for such services. At age seventy, arthritis in his hands prevented him from doing fine electrical work, so he began taking meals to homebound elders and giving rides to those who had no transportation to church on Sunday mornings. At age eighty, Jim was living in a nursing home and confined to a wheelchair with sores on both feet due to bad circulation. Jim refused to focus on his problems and instead concentrated on people around him. He took time to listen to and encourage other residents at the home and helped the nursing staff watch the front door to keep patients with Alzheimer's disease from wandering outside. Jim's special gift in his forties was his electrical skills, in his seventies it was his mobility and ability to drive a car, and in his eighties it was his friendly, outgoing, helpful attitude.

Sally's story is similar. In her forties and fifties she was an English teacher in high school. During those years, she volunteered to help organize and teach Sunday school. When she had time, Sally tutored slow-learning children from poor families in her church who could not afford private tutors. In her late sixties, Sally's eyesight began to fail. This and a mild stroke affecting her left arm eventually forced her to stop all formal teaching and tutoring activities. For some time, however, she continued to tutor by telephone, calling up students and helping them with their reading. She bought a speaker phone and adapted it so that she could hear the students better. Because she had a lot of time on her hands after her husband died, she also began calling shut-ins on a regular basis, listening to their problems and offering encouragement. In her late seventies, Sally's hearing began to fail, making it impossible for her to use the telephone, even after maximum correction with a hearing aid. Sally's eyesight had also worsened to the point that she could barely make out faces. Nevertheless, she still had an alert mind and no serious problems with walking or getting about. On Sundays a friend would pick her up and drive her to church, where she helped as a greeter. There she used her warm smile, hearty handshake, and encouraging hug (with her right arm) to make people feel welcome and cared for. Just like Jim, Sally's talent changed as she grew older; nevertheless, she continued to use whatever ability she had at the time to serve God by loving and serving others.

These cases demonstrate that God provides us with different gifts during different seasons of our lives. If we are willing, the Lord will use these abilities–no matter how small or inconsequential they may appear–to change the world in which we live. While our most obvious talents are skills we used in earlier years, sometimes the Lord takes the old abilities away and makes us aware of new talents. A willingness to serve is the most important thing on our part. Regardless of what our specific talent is, the fruits of peace, joy, and fulfillment resulting from its use remain the same. While physical health declines as we age, there is absolutely no indication that our biological capacity to experience and share the emotions of joy, peace, and happiness diminish in the least.

SUMMARY

In this chapter, we discussed how to go about identifying our special gifts and talents. We presented a Table of the different talents that people have, including the not so obvious ones. We presented several examples of persons in quite challenging circumstances who discovered and used their gifts to serve others, which ultimately brought them joy and fulfillment in their lives. We wanted to show that every one of us have a gift or talent that can be used to serve God by serving others. Finally, we stressed that our gifts and talents often change as we age and circumstances change.

DISCUSSION QUESTIONS

1. Do you feel the need for help in discovering your gifts and talents because you do not believe you have any special skills or abilities?
2. In this chapter you are offered a table of God-given gifts, talents, abilities, and skills. After reading this list, record those you think that you might possess and share them with the group.
3. Do some of the gifts and talents listed come as a surprise to you? Why and which ones?
4. In the seven case histories given, which was the most meaningful to you, and why?
5. Have you perceived that your talents, gifts, and skills have changed as your circumstances have changed with the seasons of your life? Share this process of change with the group.

6. Are you more comfortable and filled with new hope for your-self that no matter what our abilities are, God always wants us to serve him and our neighbor and will provide the ability to do so?

NOTES

1. Allen, Charles. *God's Psychiatry.* Grand Rapids, MI: Fleming H. Revell, 1953, pp. 63-66.

2. Byrd, Randolph C. Positive therapeutic effects of intercessory prayer in a coronary care unit population. *Southern Medical Journal*, 81(7), pp. 826-829, 1988.

Chapter 9

Using Our Talents

Your attitude must be like my own, for I, the Messiah, did not come to be served, but to serve.

—Matthew 20:28, LB

You, my brothers, were *called to be free.* But do not use your freedom to indulge the sinful nature; rather, serve one another in love.

—Galatians 5:13

Having identified our unique gift or talent, we must learn to use it as God intended. As discussed earlier, scriptures indicate that God has a plan for humanity in which He wants us to participate. Christ has told us that we must love God and love neighbor. Paul tells us to "excel in gifts that build up the church" (1 Corinthians 14:12). Peter says that "Each one should use whatever gift he has received to serve others, faithfully administering God's grace in its various forms" (1 Peter 4:10), and also to, ". . . gird yourselves with humility, to serve one another" (1 Peter 5:5, ASV).

Love neighbor, build up the church, serve others, be humble—these are the answers that scripture gives to the question of how we should use our gifts, those unique abilities that the Creator has given us to help achieve God's purpose. When using your gift, there are three things to bear in mind: (1) be prepared to make the necessary effort to put your talent into action; (2) realize the importance of your talent for your particular situation; and (3) always use your talent with love, kindness, and humility toward those you serve. We will now discuss each of these points.

91

First, it is not easy to mobilize one's ability and use it to minister to the needs of others. Often it takes an effort. Forces both outside and within yourself will block your path. Jesus said that if he were persecuted, we would be too. It takes persistence and perseverance to continue in the face of persecution. At times, the external barriers to carrying out your gift will be so high as to seem unsurmountable. At other times, you will not feel the energy, motivation, or inspiration to continue to serve. You will have to fight against yourself to continue on. You will become discouraged and fail often. Nevertheless, listen carefully to what Paul says:

> Do you not know that in a race all the runners run, but only one gets the prize? Run in such a way as to get the prize. (1 Corinthians 9:24).

What does Paul do?

> Therefore I do not run like a man running aimlessly; I do not fight like a man beating the air. No, I beat my body and make it my slave so that . . . I myself will not be disqualified for the prize. (1 Corinthians 9:26, 27)

We, too, must make the effort, discipline ourselves, and strive to overcome those forces that would keep our talents and abilities buried and useless to God (see Chapter 11). Discernment and wisdom, however, are of utmost importance as we use our gifts. Jesus instructs us to be "wise as serpents and gentle as doves" as we go out into the world to love and serve him.

Second, we must realize just how important, valuable, and powerful our gift is for the unique and special circumstances we are in. We cannot discount our God-given talent or ability as not being important or worthy. This attitude will drain our motivation and discourage us from making use of what we have. Remember that the size or importance of your gift or talent does not depend on you. You did not do anything to earn it, that is why it is called a gift. God chose this gift for you. What you do with the gift, however big or small, does depend on you. If you use your gift, then you can experience all the benefits and joys that anyone could possibly experience by using their gift.

For example, if your gift is physical health that enables you to serve someone by mowing a lawn or taking out garbage, and you use this gift with humility, gratefulness, and an attitude of serving the Lord, then there is no psychological or spiritual benefit that is not potentially yours. The greatest preacher, most intelligent and charismatic leader, or most talented singer, cannot experience any greater fulfillment than you can. All humans have the same capacity for experiencing the fruits of the Spirit. We are all equal in this regard. So the size or seeming importance of your ability or talent does not matter. The only thing that matters is what you do with it. It also makes absolutely no sense to desire someone else's talent. This is like saying that God does not know what he is doing, and that the other person's talent will give you more joy and fulfillment in your situation than your talent—both of which are simply not true.

> But each man has his own gift from God; one has this gift, another has that. (1 Corinthians 7:7)

> We have different gifts, according to the grace given us. (Romans 12:6)

Jesus gave us the parable of the talents to encourage us to use the gift he has given us, regardless of how big or small we think it is (Matthew 25:15-28). We all know how the story goes.

> To one he gave five talents of money, to another two talents, and to another one talent, each according to his ability.

> The man who received the five talents went at once and put his money to work and gained five more. So also, the one with the two talents gained two more.

> But the man who had received the one talent went off, dug a hole in the ground and hid his master's money.

> "Well done, good and faithful servant" [the man said to the each of his servants who had used their talents and doubled them] . . .

> [To the servant who buried his talent, however, the man said] "You wicked, lazy servant! . . . Take the talent from him and give it to the one who has the ten talents."

In this story, the boss took into account the abilities of the servants. The third servant could have doubled his talent like the other two, but he was lazy and had very little self-confidence. He probably thought, "What can I possibly do with this measly one talent? I'll just protect it. It's not enough to be able to do anything else." We have to be careful not to fall into similar traps.

The following story is quoted by Tim Hansel in *You Gotta Keep Dancin'* (LifeJourney Books, 1985), a marvelous little book about how to decide to be joyful in every situation. While the story is a bit long, we think it beautifully illustrates how some people, despite difficult circumstances, can use their talent to make life meaningful to those around them. It also illustrates the darker side of human nature that arises from a failure to appreciate our own gift and, instead, yearn for the gifts of others.

> There were once two men, both seriously ill, in the same small room of a great hospital. Quite a small room, just large enough for the pair of them—two beds, two bedside lockers, a door opening on the hall, and one window looking out on the world.
>
> One of the men, as part of his treatment, was allowed to sit up in bed for an hour in the afternoon (something to do with draining the fluid from his lungs), and his bed was next to the window.
>
> But the other man had to spend all his time flat on his back, and both of them had to be kept quiet and still, which was the reason they were in the small room by themselves, and they were grateful for peace and privacy—none of the bustle and clatter and prying eyes of the general ward for them.
>
> Of course, one of the disadvantages of their condition was that they weren't allowed to do much: no reading, no radio, certainly no television—they just had to keep quiet and still, just the two of them.
>
> Well, they used to talk for hours and hours—about their wives, their children, their homes, their jobs, their hobbies, their childhood, what they did during the war, where they'd been on vacations—all that sort of thing. Every afternoon, when the man in the bed next to the window was propped up for his hour, he would pass the time by describing what he could see outside. And the other man began to live for those hours.

The window apparently overlooked a park, with a lake, where there were ducks and swans, children throwing them bread and sailing model boats, and young lovers walking hand in hand beneath the trees, and there were flowers and stretches of grass, games of softball, people taking their ease in the sunshine, and right at the back, behind the fringe of trees, a fine view of the city skyline.

The man on his back would listen to all of this, enjoying every minute–how a child nearly fell into the lake, how beautiful the girls were in their summer dresses, then an exciting ball game, or a boy playing with his puppy. It got to the place that he could almost see what was happening outside.

Then one fine afternoon, when there was some sort of parade, the thought struck him: Why should the man next to the window have all the pleasure of seeing what was going on? Why shouldn't he get the chance?

He felt ashamed, and tried not to think like that, but the more he tried, the worse he wanted a change. He'd do anything!

In a few days, he had turned sour. *He* should be by the window. And he brooded, and couldn't sleep, and grew even more seriously ill–which none of the doctors understood.

One night as he stared at the ceiling, the other man suddenly woke up, coughing and choking, the fluid congesting in his lungs, his hand groping for the button that would bring the night nurse running. But the man watched without moving.

The coughing racked the darkness–on and on–choked off–then stopped–the sound of breathing stopped–and the man continued to stare at the ceiling.

In the morning the day nurse came in with water for their baths and found the other man dead. They took away his body, quietly, no fuss.

As soon as it seemed decent, the man asked if he could be moved to the bed next to the window. And they moved him, tucked him in, and made him quite comfortable, and left him alone to be quiet and still.

The minute they'd gone, he propped himself up on one elbow, painfully and laboriously, and looked out the window.

It faced a blank wall.[1]

No gift is more or less useful than any other. The important thing is that you recognize, value, and use the talent that you have been given. The one you have is the one that is most powerful in advancing God's kingdom in the particular and crucial position in which God has placed you. No one else in the world has ever been or will ever be in the particular place that you are in now. Do not let your chance pass by to play a vital role in advancing God's kingdom. As noted in Chapter 8, even when we lose the ability to think and reason, God can still use us to bring spiritual maturity to those around us.

Third, regardless of what our talent is, St. Paul tells us that we need to be sure we use it in a loving, sensitive, kind manner. Otherwise, all our efforts are worthless.

> If I speak in the tongues of men and of angels, but have not love, I am only a resounding gong or a clanging cymbal.
>
> If I have the gift of prophecy and can fathom all mysteries and all knowledge, and if I have a faith that can move mountains, but have not love, I am nothing.
>
> If I give all I possess to the poor and surrender my body to the flames, but have not love, I gain nothing. (1 Corinthians 13:1-3)

No matter how important we think our gift is, not matter how great or small our ability, no matter how much effort we make to serve God and serve others, if we do not do it with love and compassion, then we "gain nothing."

We recognize, however, that serving and loving others will be easier for some than for others. One person seems to love and care for others so easily and naturally–seemingly without effort. Other persons have a difficult time with this. Only with great strain and willpower can they disregard their own immediate needs and focus on the needs of others. Even then, they do not feel much (except perhaps impatience). Others have difficulty expressing love and concern for others. These individuals may be more introverted and prefer thinking and dreaming over interacting with people. Some may even feel fearful of others, afraid that they will be rejected and hurt. Much of this has to do with a person's temperament, the inherited predispositions and tendencies with which people are born. God knows this too, and has considered it when bestowing their special gifts or talents. Whatever our temperament, every one of us needs to serve others with love and kindness.

The first book of John reminds us where our love must come from in order to serve others in the way God intends:

> Dear friends, let us love one another, for love comes from God. (1 John 4:7)

> This is love; not that we loved God, but that he loved us and sent his Son as an atoning sacrifice for our sins. Dear friends, since God so loved us, we also ought to love one another. (1 John 4:10-11)

> We love because he first loved us. (1 John 4:19)

This type of love–unconditional love–comes from God, not from our devising and human effort. God loves us first. But to receive this love, we must draw near to God (Chapter 7), opening ourselves up to experience God's love. In this way we acquire the capacity to love others. It is only God's love, then, that enables us to love others.

Loving in this way does not cause fear or a sense of vulnerability: "There is no fear in love. But *perfect* [unconditional] love drives out fear" (1 John 4:18). As we unconditionally love and serve others, responding to the love that God has filled us with, then fear, anxiety, insecurity will leave. Why? Because we are no longer on the defensive–afraid we will say or do something that will cause people to hurt us or withdraw their love from us. We love others not because of what we can get from them, but because of what God has done for us and because of our love for God. This removes the fear of being hurt and rejected by others. We are hurt only when we do not get what we want in return for the love we give. That is not unconditional or "perfect" love, but rather the old barter system (I will love you, but only if you love me). Yes, in the barter system you are vulnerable and easily hurt. Not so with God's type of love.

Unconditional love, one of the "fruits of the spirit" (Galatians 5:22) calls for much more than the expression of our feelings. By definition, unconditional love means loving others without conditions attached. It means loving regardless of how you feel. When God has met your deepest emotional needs, you become free to love in this way. Love becomes an action based on a *decision*, not a feeling. Part of loving involves being sensitive to the needs of those we serve. We need to carefully study and learn about their previous life experiences, current situations, and future hopes and dreams. Only with such knowledge can we truly meet their needs in a respectful, meaningful, and sensitive manner. Otherwise, they will feel like we are simply *using them* to meet our need to serve, which will understandably make them resentful, angry, and probably cause them to reject our help.

HELPING OTHERS FIND THEIR GIFT

When using your gift to help others, it is important to remember that they, too, need to identify and use their special gift if they are to be happy and feel useful.

> Let us think of one another and how we can encourage one another to love and do good deeds. (Hebrews 10:24)

Doing things for others can make others dependent on us and rob them of self-esteem. Helping persons to discover their hidden talents, and then encouraging and making a way for them to use those talents within the framework of their current situation, is real help that will produce lasting results. The old saying, "Give a man a fish, and tomorrow he will go hungry; teach a man to fish, and tomorrow he will feed himself," is the basis for true love and respect for others. Of course, one must be cautious not to give advice when it is not wanted or when the timing is wrong. One runs the risk of being one of "Job's advisors." They thought they had all the answers, but they only increased Job's burden. Nevertheless, there are subtle and sensitive ways that you can encourage and direct others to use their talent to love and serve those around them.

For example, you are visiting a disabled shut-in, Mary, to provide emotional support and perform some practical needs for her. In your conversation with Mary, you might begin talking about Ruth who is much worse off than Mary is, and then suggest "out of the blue" that Mary call Ruth and encourage her–because "You (Mary) can really understand Ruth's situation out of your own experience." If Mary crochets, you might buy her some yarn to enable her to make a bedcover or sweater for Ruth, and then once finished, take Mary over to Ruth's place to present it to her. Just as with Mary, you would encourage Ruth to discover her special gift or talent and help her to use it. The result is that everyone learns to use his or her gifts in a mutual way to love and serve each other, discovers that each person has a role and purpose in God's great plan, and experiences the emotional and spiritual benefits of such service.

SUMMARY

In this chapter, we examined how to use our special gifts and talents. First, we stressed that using our talent might require considerable effort on our part and that we should be prepared for this. Second, we emphasized that God has uniquely fashioned our talent for the situation we are in, and that it is unwise to desire the talents or gifts of others. Third, we stressed the need to use our gift with love, kindness, humility, and respect for the person we are serving. Part of loving involves being sensitive to the other person's situation at this time in their life. This requires that we get to know the person, taking the time to learn about their past life experiences, current situation, and dreams for the future. Finally, we discussed how important it was for us to help others discover their own special gifts and talents so that they, too, can experience the benefits of loving and serving.

DISCUSSION QUESTIONS

1. Having identified your gifts, are you using them now to serve others? If so, in what way?
2. The mature years bring with them various kinds of losses, especially the loss of a spouse. In your grief have you found a bereavement group that has been helpful? For the sake of others, share how such a group can be helpful.
3. Physical disability can be another aspect of the mature years. If you or your spouse have suffered such a major disability,

how were you able to manage, find and use your gifts in spite of the circumstances? Sharing this with the group can be helpful to those who may be suffering with the same problem.

4. Have you experienced that the gift of God's unconditional love to others has sustained you in your ministry, in spite of the way you might feel about others and yourself? Has this gift of love from God energized your life?

5. What do you think about our need to be sensitive and respectful toward those we are serving? What does this involve?

6. Have you observed God's gifts to others and helped them to recognize, develop and use them to serve others? Will you share an example?

NOTE

1. Target, G.W. The window. From *The Window and Other Essays*. Nampa, ID: Pacific Press Publishing Association, pp. 5-7, 1973. Reprinted by permission.

Chapter 10

Fulfilling Our Deepest Needs

We have learned that God has equipped us with unique and special abilities for our particular circumstances in life. In this chapter we will see how loving God and loving thy neighbor using our abilities and talents can help meet the psychological and spiritual needs listed in Chapter 5.

NEEDS RELATED TO SELF

1. *A need for meaning and purpose.* Sources of meaning and purpose that depend on "health, wealth, and love from others" become more fragile and subject to loss and change as we age. Spiritual sources of meaning and purpose, on the other hand, are more constant. When devout Christians become disabled and dependent on others, lose their financial security, and are left without friends, their lives should continue to have purpose and meaning. Purpose and meaning would come from their serving God with whatever abilities or talents they still had.

What if I lose all my abilities and talents? Our assumption from the start of this book was that if you are alive here on planet Earth today, then God has a calling on your life. If the Lord takes one gift away, God has plenty more with which to replace it. Everything depends on your attitude. If you want to serve God, then God will provide the gift. It may not be the one you ordered, but it will be the best one for your situation. It may be something you never thought of as a talent or ability. God chose Moses, who had a speech defect, to be the spokesperson, for the entire Israelite nation.

As far as God is concerned, *you are God's Moses to the people that surround you.* Your special gift may be your ability to smile. It may be your capacity to show appreciation. It may be your ability to pray. If you use it to serve God, your life will have purpose and meaning because you will be participating in the greatest enterprise this world has ever known and will ever know—God's plan for humanity. You will see powerful changes in your environment as a result of your obedience to and trust in God. The impossible will happen. Just try it and see. One of the best things about the Christian life are these surprises that God blesses us with.

2. *A need for a sense of usefulness.* Many aging persons feel that their lives are useless. In all honesty, this is probably true. If our existence does not make a difference in anyone's life, then we probably will not be experiencing much satisfaction and joy. It is more important that we face the truth than try to make up reasons why we should feel useful when, in fact, we are not. This only disguises the problem. Denying that you have cancer, when you actually have it, does not help anyone. If you are told straight up that you have cancer, then you have a chance to do something about it. The same thing goes for what we are talking about. Feelings of uselessness, lack of meaning, boredom, and so forth, often have a reason for being there.[1] These feelings should prompt us to search for the special ability that God has given us to make a difference in others' lives. Doing so will help give our lives meaning and purpose and will make us feel useful.

A living, active religious faith is a powerful antidote for feelings of boredom and uselessness. You are never useless to God. God needs you and wants to recruit you. The Lord does not care how old you are, how sick you are, how tired you are, or even how little faith you have. God wants you to use whatever little faith and strength you have. None of Jesus' disciples were particularly talented, skilled, or educated. Their faith in Jesus was weak. They deserted him and denied him. Despite this, Christ used them to change the world in which they lived. Even after repeatedly failing, they were willing to get back up and follow him. God had a purpose for their lives and has a purpose for yours too.

Nevertheless, you have the freedom to choose whether or not to follow and serve God. If you do not use the gift or talent the Lord has given you, then it simply will not be used. Whatever great things God had planned to do through you cannot take place. And you will probably have to experience whatever feelings that follow as a result of this decision. They may include feeling useless. *But it does not have to be that way.* You are not locked into a situation with no escape. God has provided one for you. Decide to take it!

3. *A need for vision.* Catching God's vision for our lives can fill and overflow them with meaning and purpose until the hour we are called home. The Lord has a much bigger vision for our lives than we do. God sees each of us as playing an instrumental role in the Creator's great plan for humanity. Again, without our service, the kingdom cannot advance in the little area of the world where God has placed us. Wherever you are, your life is literally affecting hundreds of people each week–if not directly, then by the effects you are having indirectly through the people with whom you do have contact.

For example, suppose you are a patient in a hospital or even a nursing home. If you are pleasant, smile, and show appreciation for the care a nurse is providing to you, this may help her day go better and she will be nicer to other people for whom she cares. Each of those people may treat their family members who visit them a little nicer, who then go back to their jobs and treat their co-workers better, and so on and so forth. Before you know it, you have affected the lives of dozens of people, many of whom you do not even know about. These effects will extend not only to your generation but to the generations that will follow you–your children and grandchildren–who are watching you respond to the trials in your life. Whether you like it or not, you are their role model. Consciously or unconsciously, they are taking cues from you on how to deal with situations and respond to others in their lives.

When you begin to see how important you are in God's plan, your life will become more exciting than it has ever been. As you obey God's call in your life, you will be surprised day after day. The unpleasant colleague who mistreats you at work will begin to change. You will be talking with the relative who you have not spoken to in five years, and even enjoy it! You will see a change in the negative attitude of the grumpy nurses aide who gives you your bath each week. Your life will become thrilling again as you catch God's vision for you.

4. *A need for hope.* If there is one word that describes the outcome of having a relationship with God, that word is *hope.* Even in the

bleakest of circumstances, a strong faith provides hope. Remember Paul's words quoted earlier. "And we know that all things work together for good to them that love God, to them who are *the called* according to his purpose" (Romans 8:28, KJV). You are the called! Everything that happens to you—no matter how bad it may seem—can be turned into something good, if you desire to serve God using your gifts. Every negative event or experience can be used to advance God's kingdom on earth and fulfill the vision that God has for your life. Unless you act on faith, however, you will miss the good.

Faith provides hope in other ways. Faith opens up the possibility that God may miraculously heal a disease or illness with which you have been diagnosed, or faith will help you cope with it better. Even death itself cannot take away this hope, for as Christians we look forward to an eternity of joy and happiness in the presence of our Lord who loves us. "Where, O death, is your victory? Where, O death, is your sting?" (1 Corinthians 15:55, referring to Hosea 13:14). As we serve others, our love and compassion will not only give them hope, but will increase our hope as well. "A liberal man will be enriched, and one who waters will himself be watered" (Proverbs 11:25, RSV).

5. *A need for support in coping with loss and change.* As we love and serve God, the impact of losses in our lives is made easier. This does not mean that we will not get upset or experience emotional pain when a loved one dies or when we experience a serious physical illness that is painful or disabling. It only means that these events will not *dominate or control our lives.* No longer is our sense of identity determined by our physical health, material possessions, or even relationships with others (particularly those of the barter type discussed earlier). Instead, our identity is rooted in our relationship with God, which becomes the source of fulfillment for all our needs. Nothing that life throws our way can threaten this. Jesus said, "But store up for yourselves treasures in heaven, where moth and rust do not destroy, and where thieves do not break in and steal" (Matthew 6:20). Furthermore, loving and serving others in their time of need will result in their wanting to return this favor when your own or someone else's need comes.

6. *A need to adapt to increasing dependency.* If our vision and goal in life is to love and serve God by serving others, then becom-

ing more dependent on others should not be too threatening. Granted, it may take some effort learning to serve God in a different way than that to which we were accustomed. Nevertheless, dependency will not end all possibility of our experiencing the fruits of the Spirit or of a full, complete life, as it might for someone whose hope and value depends on their independence and self-sufficiency.

We have shown this in several previous cases. The recently disabled person who is committed to serving God now has an opportunity to serve the persons taking care of him or her. The case of Sarah in Chapter 8 illustrates several ways that dependent persons can serve God by serving their caretakers. In this way, God can open up a whole field of service for disabled persons that will give their lives meaning and purpose and will truly advance God's kingdom.

7. *A need to transcend difficult circumstances.* For Christians who have decided to commit their lives to God, there are no circumstances that cannot be transcended. There is no situation so difficult that it cannot be transformed into an opportunity to serve and yield the emotional and spiritual fruit thereof. Nobody said that it would be easy, but it is possible.

> So we fix our eyes not on what is seen, but on what is unseen. For what is seen is temporary, but what is unseen is eternal (. . .). We live by faith, not by sight. (2 Corinthians 4:18, 5:7)

> And we know that *all things* work together for good to them that love God, to them who are the called according to his purpose. (Romans 8:28, KJV)

Our meaning and purpose in life does not come from our circumstances. The focus of our faith—our ultimate concern—has nothing to do with our living arrangements, health status, material possessions, job, or social position. We live in order to serve God, and we can do this no matter what situation we are in—because God will make a way. Even as death approaches, we are serving our Lord, concerned about the welfare and emotional well-being of those around us. Our future is secure, and nothing in this world can threaten it. As Paul said,

> I am convinced that neither death nor life, neither angels nor demons, neither the present nor the future, nor any powers,

neither height or depth nor anything else in all creation, will be able to separate us from the love of God that is in Christ Jesus our Lord. (Romans 8:38)

For none of us lives to himself alone and none of us dies to himself alone. If we live, we live to the Lord; and if we die, we die to the Lord. So, whether we live or die, we belong to the Lord. (Romans 14:7-8)

8. *A need for personal dignity.* Many persons base their view of themselves on their position in society, the status of their job, how much money they make, with whom they associate, type of car they drive or neighborhood in which they live. Others make this estimation of themselves based on what they have accomplished in their lives, or on the types of relationships they have. Still others base their dignity on how people treat them, on how much others respect them. These are all weak and shaky grounds for self-esteem. Scriptures provide a basis for true worth that goes far beyond anything that we ourselves could ever earn:

What do you think? If a man owns a hundred sheep, and one of them wanders away, will he not leave the ninety-nine on the hills and go to look for the one that wandered off? And if he finds it, I tell you the truth, he is happier about that one sheep than about the ninety-nine that did not wander off. In the same way your Father in heaven is not willing that any of these little ones [that's us!] should be lost. (Matthew 18:12-14)

Because you are sons, God sent the Spirit of his Son into our hearts, the Spirit who calls out, "*Abba*, Father." So you are no longer a slave, but a son; since you are a son, God has made you also an heir. (Galatians 4:6-7)

He chose to give us birth through the word of truth, that we might be a kind of firstfruits of all he created. (James 1:18)

Our true dignity lies not in what we have done, or in how others treat us, but in what *God has done for us* because of his mercy and grace. We are made in the Creator's very own image (Genesis 1:26-27). God has called our bodies "temples of the Holy Spirit." This means that God actually lives within us (1 Corinthians 3:16, 2 Corinthians 6:16). The Lord has called us "children," "sons," "heirs" to God's throne and kingdom (Romans 8:14-17; Galatians 4:6). God has given us the whole earth and instructed us to master it (Genesis 2:28-30; Psalm 8:3-8). If this doesn't give you true value and worth, then nothing can. Because our personal dignity comes from God, who or what can threaten it? Only God can take it away. And Christ has said that he loves us, and has proven it by dying for us. God has given us a true basis for personal dignity. We can now love and serve the Lord out of gratefulness for this great gift.

If God is for us, who can be against us? (Romans 8:31)

9. *A need to express feelings.* When bad things happen to us, we ask the question, "Why?" We often ask this question of God. As we have noted before, this is completely natural and normal. Scriptures provide ample precedent for questioning God and the expression of negative feelings (Psalm 10:15; 37:35-36; 55:15; 58:1-11; 69:19-28; 73:1-17; 83:1-18; 109:1-20; Jeremiah 12:1-4). Such meditations and prayers produce a healthy catharsis. Take also the case of Job, whom the Bible describes as a *perfect* man.

There was a man in the land of Uz, whose name was Job; and that man was *perfect* and upright, and one that feared God, and eschewed evil. (Job 1:1, KJV)

When things turned bad, however, Job got mad at God and passionately wished he had never been born. If anyone ever expressed negative feelings toward God, Job did. And yet the Creator responded to Job's angry questions by giving him an experience of God's own presence—an experience so incredible that Job replied in awe,

I was talking about things I knew nothing about and did not understand, things far too wonderful for me . . . *I had heard about you before, but now I have seen you* . . . (Job 42:3,5, LB)

Obviously, God can handle even our most angry and hateful feelings. Feelings like this should not arouse guilt because they are normal and necessary. However, after spending a time being angry and questioning, we must move beyond it–otherwise, this will block the comfort that God can provide for healing. As we listen to others express their questions and anger at God, and help them work through these feelings, our own troubles and unanswered questions will not seem as important.

10. *A need to be thankful.* While some people seem to be just naturally thankful for the good things in their lives, most of us must *learn* to be thankful. This may require that we search hard for things to be thankful about, and make an effort to be thankful for even the small things. Scriptures emphasize that thankfulness does not come naturally, but is an attitude learned through *practice.* Paul said: ". . . I have *learned* to be content whatever the circumstances" (Philippians 4:11). Learning to be thankful involves remembering and praising God for the gifts, blessings, and even the trials that are allowed to come into our lives to make us who we are. The consequences of remembering and being thankful are beautifully summarized below:

> Praise the Lord, O my soul,
> and forget not all his benefits
> who forgives all your sins
> and heals all our diseases,
> who redeems your life from the pit
> and crowns you with love and compassion,
> who satisfies your desires with good things
> So that your youth is renewed like the eagle's.
> (Psalm 103:2-5)

Being thankful actually renews our youth and health–brings energy and joy back into our lives. Failure to do so, on the other hand, will cause us to feel dissatisfied, drain us of energy and excitement, and probably make us feel old and sick. As we love and serve God by seeking to meet the needs of those less fortunate around us, we begin to see how blessed we truly are. Remembering to appreciate and be thankful for our unique, special God-given gifts will double the psychological benefits that using these gifts will yield. Not only will there be satisfaction because we are in God's will, serving the Lord, and extending God's kingdom on earth, but being thankful will add another layer of joy to the whole affair (Hebrews 13:15-16; Thessalonians 5:16-18).

11. *A need for continuity with the past.* In a world that is rapidly changing, aging persons need something that helps maintain continuity from childhood, through young adulthood, into middle age and the later years. A strong relationship with God provides such continuity. The Bible depicts God as showing "no variation or shadow due to change" (James 1:17, RSV), promising that the Lord will be "with you always, to the very end of the age" (Matthew 28:20). God says to us "Even to your old age, I shall be the same, And even to your graying years I shall bear you!" (Isaiah 46:4, ASV). Such assurances bring a sense of comfort, peace, and continuity.

The Bible itself is the same Bible that our parents or grandparents read to us when we were small children, even if we use a different translation, and it is the same Bible that we read to our children and grandchildren. The great hymns sung in church and familiar rituals and prayers, even in churches far distant from our home church, remain much the same as when we were small. In these ways, a strong faith maintains both internal and external continuity in our lives, arousing (as it did in years past) feelings of devotion, of belonging, of being a part of something which is timeless and much greater than ourselves. Likewise, as we love and serve God by bearing the burdens of brothers and sisters who surround us, we carry on a great tradition that Christ role-modeled for us 2,000 years ago. This service produces the same fruit in our lives, no matter where we are or what our changing circumstances might be.

12. *A need to accept and prepare for death and dying.* Such is the time when we need to know and feel that God is with us, caring and sharing this experience.

> Out of my distress I call on the Lord; the Lord answered me and set me free. With the Lord on my side to help me I do not fear. (Psalm 118:5-6)

> For this God is our God for ever and ever: he will be our guide even unto death. (Psalm 48:14)

As God's servants, we are assured of the Lord's presence and blessings when we are called home:

> For none of us lives to himself alone and none of us dies to
> himself alone. If we live, we live to the Lord; and if we die, we
> die to the Lord. So, whether we live or die, we belong to the Lord.
> (Romans 14:7-8)

> For to me, to live is Christ and to die is gain. If I am to go on
> living in the body, this will mean fruitful labor for me. Yet what
> shall I choose? I do not know! I am torn between the two: I
> desire to depart and be with Christ, which is better by far . . .
> (Philippians 1:21-23)

> Then I heard a voice from heaven say, "Write: Blessed are the
> dead who die in the Lord from now on." "Yes," says the Spirit,
> "they will rest from their labor, for their deeds will follow them."
> (Revelations 14:13)

Every day we have an opportunity to help others and serve our
Lord, and how often we miss it! Let knowledge of the certainty of
our death someday accomplish one thing: to motivate us to serve
Christ now and every day God grants us here on earth.

NEEDS RELATED TO GOD

13. *A need to be certain that God exists.* Can we know that God
exists? Jesus said, "I am the Good Shepherd and know my sheep,
and they *know* me . . . " (John 10:14). This suggests that God's
sheep, the people who follow God's teachings, actually come to
know that God is. How does this come about? Again, Jesus tells us:

> If you hold to my teachings, you are really my disciples.
> Then you will know the truth, and the truth will set you free.
> (John 8:31-32)

In other words, if we follow Christ's teachings, then we will *know*
the truth. And what is the truth? It is Jesus Christ, who says "I am
the way and *the truth* and the life . . . " (John 14:6). Thus, truth is a

person. We can know that God exists by knowing God's son, Jesus Christ. And we come to know him by following his teachings: to love God with our whole heart, soul, mind, and strength and to love our neighbor as our self—in other words, to love and serve God by serving others. By doing this, we will come to know that God exists, for *we will experience the Creator working through us.*

14. *A need to believe that God is on our side.* Again, Jesus promises us in Matthew 25:34-40 to personally welcome us into his kingdom. Toward the end of that Gospel, Jesus again assures us, "and be SURE of this—that I am with you always, even to the end of the world" (Matthew 28:20, LB). Listen to the experience of the Psalmist, "The Lord is my shepherd, I shall not want (. . .). Yea, though I walk through the valley of the shadow of death, I will fear no evil: for *thou art with me*; thy rod and thy staff they comfort me" (Psalm 23:1,4, KJV). In our hour of true need, God will be so close to us that we will be able to feel the holy rod and staff, which will give us comfort. What a beautiful vision! And again, "For this God is our God for ever and ever: he will be our guide even unto death" (Psalm 48:14, KJV). If we commit our lives to the Lord, God will never leave our sides.

15. *A need to experience God's presence.* Many people do not feel God's presence in their lives. They believe that God exists because their parents told them so, or because others around them believe, or because they are afraid not to believe. Some, however, believe because they have experienced God's presence and power. This is due to God's grace which is available to every one of us. We need to take time to pray and talk with God, worship and praise God, and respond to God's gentle urging. By *doing these things*, we will come to experience God's presence, power, and love in our lives. We can never, however, really experience God until we humble ourselves and recognize that we cannot do this on our own. Without grace, we would never have known that we even needed to. Sometimes this grace comes in the form of pain and suffering—and it is there that God meets us. Many times God's grace comes to us as we comfort those who are experiencing pain and suffering (2 Corinthians 1:3-7).

16. *A need to experience God's unconditional love.* This is how God loves each of us. Just as a mother loves her small, precious baby,

so does the Lord love you and me as sons or daughters. The Lord's love for us exceeds even a mother's love:

> Can a mother forget the baby at her breast and have no compassion on the child she has born? *Though she may forget, I will not forget you.* (Isaiah 49:15)

What a picture of God's tender concern for us. Think about it. Is this not Someone who is worthy of our worship, our devotion, our unswerving service? While God can and often does bestow this love directly on us, most of the time our Lord chooses to show the world love through our actions. We are God's instruments of unconditional love. As we serve and love others unconditionally, we ourselves experience more fully the Lord's unconditional love for us.

17. *A need to pray alone, with others, and for others.* As we love God with our whole mind, soul, and strength, we begin to desire to communicate and spend time with our Lord. As we love and serve others, we will need the strength and wisdom that staying in touch with God provides. God gives us the power to love and directions on how to love when we meditate on scripture and pray. Most of the time we do not know how to meet the needs of others or even what those needs are. But God does know, and wants us to know.

We need to prepare ourselves so that we can hear God through the hustle and bustle of our daily lives. This requires a quiet time when we empty our minds of worldly thoughts and focus entirely on God. We often need to do this alone. At times, however, God will not speak to us when we are alone, but will instead wait until we are praying with others.

Serving our neighbors by praying for them fills a deep need that God has placed within us. It provides us with a powerful tool that enables us to help others in situations that would otherwise be entirely hopeless. We should never, never underestimate the power of prayer to change circumstances in our or others' lives. We should pray for them when we are alone, as well as when we are with them (if they give us permission). When you pray with them, encourage them to pray for their own needs and simply agree with them before God. Most people know their needs better than you do. In this way, you will learn how you can best serve them, and at the same time show respect and sensitivity.

18. *A need to read and be inspired by scripture.* As we said in Chapter 5, God communicates to us through Holy Scripture. The person who loves God with the whole heart, soul, and mind will find great fulfillment here. The Bible provides direction for our lives, as well as role models of men and women who served God by serving their neighbors. It contains information about the barriers they encountered and the steps that had to be taken to overcome those barriers. Loving and serving others makes us see our need for God's word in our lives, and reading God's word will make us see our need to love and serve others.

19. *A need to worship God, individually and corporately.* Loving and serving others is a form of worship. We do so because of our appreciation and love for God, because we know that such actions honor God. We also need time for the refreshing that comes from corporate worship, from the fellowship of others who are also trying to love and serve God with their lives. It is often in these assemblies that God's presence and power is felt the strongest. As we receive communion during the service, we Christians remember how much Jesus gave up for us, how much he suffered for us, how much he loves us. As we serve others and suffer with them, we are truly followers of Christ, and our worship will take on much deeper meaning.

20. *A need to love and serve God.* To those who are weary of serving their possessions, their appetites, or their relationships, Christ beckons, "Take my yoke upon you and learn from me, for I am gentle and humble in heart, and you will find rest for your souls. For my yoke is easy and my burden is light" (Matthew 11:29-30). As we have said before, serving God is always easier than taking on the burdens that our human nature and social pressures wish us to carry. Serving others for God's sake brings so much more fulfillment than we could ever obtain by obsessively focusing on ourselves and our needs.

NEEDS RELATED TO OTHERS

21. *A need for fellowship with others.* Fellowship with God on an intimate, personal level can dispel loneliness–yet not completely. The Creator has chosen not to completely fill this need for fellowship. God does not want us to be totally independent of others. While this may

seem like a contradiction of what we said before, it is not. We need other people to give us feedback, to provide a check on our lives and on the directions we are taking. This does not mean that we should be dependent on others in preference to God, who is our ultimate source of stability. It means that God has called us to be in fellowship with each other, to love and care for each other in a mutual way. We are the "body of Christ"–each part interdependent on all the other parts and taking direction from the head (1 Corinthians 12:27).

22. *A need to love and serve others.* If we are loving God with our whole heart and soul and being filled by God's love, then we have a natural desire to want to share this love with others. We become a fountain of God's love that flows toward others. Again, God–not ourselves–is the source of this love, concern, and compassion that is other-directed. Without God's overflowing love, we are self-centered and want others to center their attention on us as well. Not so for the followers of Christ (Matthew 20:26-28). Our call is to serve and direct attention away from ourselves, to God. When we respond, we become co-creators with God of the good that results.

23. *A need to confess and be forgiven.* Because we are all sinners, we need God's forgiveness. Before we can be forgiven, we must admit to our wrongdoing and humbly confess to God–without excuse or rationalization. When we empty ourselves of pride and self-importance, we are ready to serve and be used. Scriptures emphasize this over and over again. Confession is the start of new beginnings. This is best exemplified in Jesus' parable of the prodigal son. The turning point in the story is when the son acknowledges his circumstances and need: "I will arise and go to my Father, and I will say to him, 'Father I have sinned against heaven and before you; I am no longer worthy to be your son . . .'" His father's response illustrates how readily God accepts us as we turn back: ". . . this my son was dead, and is alive again; he was lost, and is found" (Luke 15:18-24, KJV). In order to truly love and serve others, we must confess our sins against them, even if this is only a sin of attitude, and forgive them for whatever things they may have done to harm or disappoint us. This includes their not responding as we would expect to our love, or even the rejection of our love.

24. *A need to forgive others.* The following story illustrates how unforgiveness can block our service to others. As part of her church

work, Mildred would visit Mrs. Willaby, a homebound elderly woman. Mrs. Willaby lived alone and was very disabled, suffering from chronic arthritis pain. Her husband died about a year before, and she was seldom visited by her children who lived in distant cities and were busy with their own lives. Mrs. Willaby's physical and emotional pain made her bitter and disagreeable. She seldom showed appreciation for Mildred's visits or for the meals that Mildred brought over. When the time came each week for her to visit Mrs. Willaby, Mildred began to feel overwhelmed with dread. She finally stopped visiting Mrs. Willaby. Even though she had started out wanting to love and serve this lady, Mildred could not continue because of the unforgiveness that built up within her in response to Mrs. Willaby's negative attitude and lack of appreciation. Once Mildred's pastor pointed this out to her, she confessed the unforgiveness and forgave Mrs. Willaby for the way she acted. Mildred asked God to give her a supernatural love for this person despite Mrs. Willaby's negative attitude, and she resumed her visits to the lady. Eventually, Mrs. Willaby softened and confessed that she really looked forward to Mildred's visits and hoped that she would never stop.

The defining characteristic of the Christian described by Jesus Christ himself is the love we show for each other (John 13:35). This includes loving those who have hurt you, rejected you, cheated you, or hurt someone you love. And yet it is so hard to forgive! Why does God demand this of us—in fact, make it the very door to our own forgiveness? It is because God loves us, and does not want to see our short lives destroyed by bitterness and resentment.

How do we forgive? Remember what Mildred did? She humbled herself before God, confessing the unforgiveness in her heart and powerlessness to deal with it (sought advice from her pastor). She asked God to give her a supernatural *love* for Mrs. Willaby, and then followed God's urging to use her gifts to continue serving Mrs. Willaby. This is often not easy, but God's love is the most powerful weapon we have. Nothing can stand up against it.

25. *A need to cope with the loss of loved ones.* Belief in and commitment to God can lessen the fear of losing others and enable us to truly love those we care for right to the end. We must remember that God loves our spouse, children, parents, and close friends

much more than we could possibly love them. As we have said before, our natural love for others is a self-centered type of love. We fear that we will lose someone who has loved us, needed us, comforted us, been a companion to us. We may even distance ourselves from them when they are sick and dying. This is a natural defense by which we make their eventual loss easier on ourselves. We disconnect from them slowly and gradually, even before they have died, which is what dying persons sense and fear the most.

God's love is other-centered, concerned about the person's eternal good and welfare. If we can begin to treat our loved ones in this way, we will not only tolerate their deaths easier, but also make their dying easier for them. Our dying loved ones need us to be fully and completely with them, not disconnected or disconnecting from them. When we trust that God has the situation completely under control and will comfort us after our loved one is gone, then we will be able to remain connected to the person, fully available when he or she really needs us at the hour of death.

SUMMARY

In this chapter we restated twenty-five of our deepest psychological and spiritual needs. We tried to show how loving God and serving others can help meet each of these basic needs. While it is possible that we can fulfill many of them in other ways, we believe that as followers of Christ, loving God and loving others is the most effective way that we can accomplish these goals. For some of us, depending on our circumstances, it may be the only way.

DISCUSSION QUESTIONS

1. What responsibility do we have as Christians to the world? How are the Christians whom you know fulfilling this responsibility? How are you?
2. How would the choice between belief that the world is all there is, versus the Christian hope of eternal life, affect a person's whole life?

3. On a scale of 1 to 10 how would you rate your adaptability to change?
4. How does God's expectation of a successful life differ from the standards of the world?
5. Do you have difficulty experiencing and identifying your feelings? If so, do you know why?
6. Is thanksgiving to God in all things a normal response in your life, or do you need to learn a better understanding of thanksgiving?
7. Twelve needs related to self are listed. Which of these do you struggle with most?
8. Eight needs related to God are listed. Which of these relate more to your life?
9. There are five needs related to others. Which of these are most applicable to you?

NOTE

1. We are assuming here that such feelings are not the result of a biological depression or other mental disorder, which often causes such feelings and needs treatment with special medication and psychotherapy.

Chapter 11

Avoiding Extremes and Burnout

Serving God by serving others will ultimately bring deep fulfillment, joy, and a sense of purpose to our lives. We have repeatedly stressed, however, that serving in this way will not be easy–even with God's help. You can expect to experience suffering as you seek to serve Christ. Jesus was "despised, and rejected of men; *a man of sorrows*, and acquainted with grief . . . " (Isaiah 53:3, ASV). If Christ suffered, then you will not be able to escape it either. There is a type of suffering, however, that can and should be avoided–the type of suffering that is exhausting and prevents you from using your gift. In this chapter, we discuss some of the barriers to using your gift that lead to burnout.[1] While we are called to bear burdens, Christ says "my yoke is easy and my burden is light" (Matthew 11:30). While serving Christ is a burden, remember that he carries the heavy end of the yoke, so our burden is a *light* one. If it is not, then something is wrong.

When using your talents to serve others, there are traps that will rob you of the psychological and spiritual benefits of this activity. If you find that you are getting tired or wearing out under a heavy yoke, ask yourself the following questions:

1. Why am I serving?
2. Whom am I serving?
3. Have I been resting?
4. Have I been sharing?
5. Do I need to set limits?
6. Do I need to persevere?

WHY AM I SERVING?

It is easy to serve our neighbors for unhealthy reasons. When caring for and ministering to the needs of others, we must repeatedly ask ourselves the question, "Why am I doing this?" Is it for social reasons? Is it to dispel my own loneliness? Is it so that others will admire and respect me? Is it for the appreciation others will show me? Is it to get "in" with the right crowd? Is it to relieve my guilt? Is it to compensate for past wrongs or other errors in my past? Is it to win God's approval, or to make up for the approval I never got as a child?

Am I doing this so that others will admire and respect me? Often, quite subtly, the appreciation and positive feedback that we receive from the persons we serve, or from our peer group, slowly become the main reasons for our actions. They begin to replace our primary motive, e.g., our calling to love and serve God. Why is this so unhealthy, you might ask. The reason is because we become dependent on how people respond to our efforts. This is an unstable position to be in because our well-being will rise and fall depending on the reactions of others. The same principle applies if we serve others in order to win their appreciation and respect. Many people do not appreciate the things we do for them, and may come to expect it. Some may even resent it. Others will try to take advantage of us or use us. Human nature makes us extraordinarily self-centered. We have powerful needs and we easily make our primary goal in life the meeting of those needs. Only with great effort can we step beyond our own needs, put ourselves in the shoes of another, and view a situation from that person's perspective. When we know God is meeting our deepest needs, this frees us to see, understand, and minister to the needs of others.

If we are serving others for social reasons such as appreciation, praise, and respect, we are setting ourselves up to feel used and unappreciated. Our unmet expectations will make us feel hurt, let down, sometimes angry and bitter toward those we serve. It certainly does not encourage the type of commitment and long-suffering that the unconditional love in 1 Corinthians 13 describes. This type of love is possible only when our *primary motivation* for loving is our dedication and commitment to God, not how others make us feel

(1 Corinthians 3:10-15). If we are serving God, then God will reward us–not the persons we are serving. Of course, it is always nice when we are loved and appreciated by those we serve. We cannot, however, depend on this to keep us going. Our emotional sustenance must come from God, who will "supply every need of yours" (Philippians 4:19, RSV) and will never disappoint us.

> Serve wholeheartedly, as if you were serving the Lord, not men, because you know that *the Lord will reward* everyone for whatever good he does . . . (Ephesians 6:7-8)

> Servants, obey in all things your masters according to the flesh; not with eyeservice, as menpleasers; but in singleness of heart, fearing God:
> And whatsoever ye do, do it heartily as to the Lord and not unto men;
> Knowing that *of the Lord ye shall receive the reward of the inheritance*; for ye serve the Lord Christ. (Colossians 3:22-24, KJV)

Next, are we serving for unhealthy psychological reasons? Are we trying to make up for some sin committed in the past? Is our service a type of penance? Is it because we are unable to forgive ourselves or accept Christ's free gift of forgiveness made possible by his death on the cross? If our actions are motivated by neurotic guilt, this may cause us to drive ourselves to extremes of activity because of our inability to satisfy this insatiable need. Serving others primarily out of guilt or to avoid emotional pain, is unwise and will not be accompanied by the joy and fulfillment that results from serving out of love, appreciation, thankfulness, and adoration for God.

Are we trying to win God's approval? This is also an unproductive incentive. As Brother Lawrence pointed out, God loves and approves us just the way we are–we are loved because of God's grace and mercy, not because of our actions or what we have done or ever will do. We do not have to serve God in order to get approval. If we are serving others to win God's approval, then we may work ourselves to death and still not feel a sense of acceptance. We must realize that we already have all of this. Then we can serve God out of our strength, not weakness, because of the gratefulness we have for all the Lord has done for us.

> But be sure to fear [respect, honor] the Lord and serve him faithfully with all your heart; consider what great things he has done for you. (1 Samuel 12:24)

WHOM AM I SERVING?

Why we are serving is closely related to *Whom* we are serving. If we are loving, caring for, ministering to the needs of another person for unhealthy social or psychological reasons, then we are not serving God. You are serving your social or psychological need. As we noted above, such service brings only temporary feelings of peace, comfort, and belonging which are fragile, easily disturbed, and in need of constant replenishing. Even serving others because of the altruistic satisfaction of seeing another person's need met or suffering relieved, does not produce the joy and peace that comes from serving God. Improvements or change in them, then, become necessary for us to feel we are doing something worthwhile. The people we serve, however, may not get better or show dramatic improvements that are expected. If they do not improve, then we feel unfulfilled and powerless, and we may even feel angry and desert them. Thus, even altruistic motivations–as wonderful as they are–may be insufficient to keep us loving and serving others when circumstances are difficult and progress is slow. Remember, the healthiest and most fulfilling type of service and love is when God–not ourselves or others–is the focus of our concern.

> And now, O Israel, what does the Lord your God ask of you but to fear the Lord your God, to walk in all his ways, to love him, to serve the Lord your God with all your heart and with all your soul . . . (Deuteronomy 10:12, see also 11:13)

> And you, my son Solomon, acknowledge the God of your father, and serve him with wholehearted devotion and with a willing mind, for the Lord searches every heart and understands every motive behind the thoughts. If you seek him, he will be found by you . . . (1 Chronicles 28:9)

Worship the Lord your God, and serve him only. (Matthew 4:10, see also Luke 4:8)

When either people or our own neurotic needs are at the focus of our concern, we are serving "idols," the false gods that scripture talks about. The consequences are often fatigue, weariness, and, ultimately, burnout.

If you violate the covenant of the Lord your God, which he commanded you, and go and *serve other gods and bow down to them*, the Lord's anger will burn against you, and you will quickly perish from the good land he has given you. (Joshua 23:16, also see 24:20)

[Those] who refuse to listen to my words, who follow the stubbornness of their hearts and *go after other gods to serve and worship them*, will be like this belt–completely useless! (Jeremiah 13:10)

If you are serving the wrong gods, then admit it and stop. Begin serving the real God, the one worthy of your devotion, and the Lord will refresh you with new purpose, energy, and hope. Christ died in order to free us from attachment to the things of this world. Christ has freed us, saved us, cleansed us, so that we can serve and become attached to God instead of worldly things. Again, this is ultimately for our own good, not God's.

If you are returning to the Lord with all your hearts, then rid yourselves of the foreign gods and the Ashtoreths and commit yourselves to the Lord and serve him only, and he will deliver you out of the hand of the Philistines. (1 Samuel 7:3)

How much more, then, will the blood of Christ, who through the eternal Spirit offered himself unblemished to God, cleanse our consciences from acts that lead to death, *so that we may serve the living God!* (Hebrews 9:14)

As we serve others with our special gifts or talents, we must constantly remember Whom we are really serving. We are serving God because by serving our neighbors we are doing what God has asked us to do. But it goes even further than that. Jesus says that we are actually serving *him* when we are serving the poor, the disadvantaged, the person in need:

> When the Son of Man comes in his heavenly glory. . . . Then the King will say to those on his right, "Come, you who are blessed by my Father; take your inheritance, the kingdom prepared for you since the creation of the world. For I was hungry and you gave me something to eat, I was thirsty and you gave me something to drink, I was a stranger and you invited me in, I needed clothes and you clothed me, I was sick and you looked after me, I was in prison and you came to visit me." Then the righteous will answer him, "Lord, when did we see you hungry and feed you, or thirsty and give you something to drink? When did we see you a stranger and invite you in, or needing clothes and clothe you? When did we see you sick or in prison and go to visit you?" The king will reply, "I tell you the truth, *whatever you did for one of the least of these brothers of mine, you did for me.*" (Matthew 25:34-40)

Think about that. What if we had the opportunity to visit Jesus and meet a need of his? Wouldn't we jump at the chance? Well, when we are serving another person we can look on that person, in all reality and truth, and say to ourselves, "I'm serving Christ!" This will renew our energy, motivation, drive, and purpose in serving.

HAVE I BEEN RESTING?

We have been encouraging you to commit yourselves to serve God by serving others. Serving in this way often energizes people. Without sufficient rest, however, serving can lead to fatigue, exhaustion, even physical illness. Remember, the commandment is "love thy neighbor *as thyself.*" As we have said before, this assumes that we are loving, respecting, and caring for ourselves and our bodies. The believer's body is a temple of the Holy Spirit (Acts 17:24-28; 1 Corinthians 3:16; 6:19; 2 Corinthians 6:16; Ephesians 2:20-22; 3;17; 1 Peter 2:5). It deserves even more attention than the places where we gather to worship. Not only do we need adequate sleep (usually seven to eight hours), but also regular exercise and proper eating habits. The Lord has also commanded us to take more extended periods of time off to rest and refresh ourselves. In the Old Testament, both the sabbath and frequent religious feasts and holidays served this purpose. In the New Testament, Jesus often reminded his disciples of their need to rest. Jesus frequently left the crowds to find a quiet place to pray, refresh himself, and receive direction from God the Father.

> This is what the Lord commanded: "Tomorrow is to be a day of rest, a holy Sabbath to the Lord." (Exodus 16:23)

> Six days you shall labor, but on the seventh day you shall rest; even during the plowing season and harvest you must rest. (Exodus 34:21)

> Then, because so many people were coming and going that they did not even have a chance to eat, he said to them, "Come with me by yourselves to a quiet place and get some rest." (Mark 6:31)

As maturing Christians, we all require a time to "be still and wait on the Lord." There are psychological and spiritual needs that cannot be met unless we take time away from serving others to contemplate and experience God in the quiet and stillness.

Taking Time Off

Planning is essential to avoid fatigue and exhaustion. We must learn to pace ourselves. Take time off on a regular basis to do things for your own enjoyment and reward—take a trip, visit the grandchildren, go to a ball game, go out to dinner, treat yourself to something special. Do not wait until you are exhausted. God wants to bless us for our faithful service. Let the Lord do it! To serve God with all our might and strength, at our greatest potential, we must be refreshed and rejuvenated. How often should we rest? That depends on your personality and particular circumstances. Some persons will require relatively little time for resting, others will require more. Rest is godly and is commanded, not an option.

If you are resting and find that you are getting bored, then you should ask yourself two questions: "Have I become addicted to serving?" and "Have I been resting too long?" If we have become addicted to serving, then we must find out why. If we cannot take a break and enjoy ourselves, then our need to serve may be extreme or compulsive. If so, our serving may be driven by one of the social or psychological needs discussed earlier, rather than our love for God. There is a time to be still, to contemplate, to receive from the Lord.

If, after a reasonable time of rest, you find yourself becoming uneasy then this may be a signal that you need to get back to serving. These are times for refreshing, for renewal, for strengthening. If we are not being refreshed, something is wrong.

Prayer and Meditation

While recreational activities may contribute to our refreshment, it is from God that true renewal comes. Thus, in addition to regular vacations, it is necessary to put aside time each day for prayer and meditation. It is God's presence that refreshes us the most.

> The Lord replied, "My Presence will go with you, and I will give you rest." (Exodus 33:14)
>
> My soul finds rest in God alone . . . (Psalm 62:1)

HAVE I BEEN SHARING?

As noted before, serving can be stressful and may require sacrifice at times. This is particularly true if our work isolates us from other Christians. We need the fellowship of other committed people with whom we can share our difficulties and burdens, as well as our joys, victories, and answered prayers. Sharing feelings of frustration, anger, disappointment, and guilt with those who understand because they are in a similar situation, can be immensely freeing. We need to encourage one another (1 Thessalonians 5:11; Hebrews 3:13). Christ emphasized the need not only for "agape" love (love with God at its focus that is unselfish and ready to serve), but also "phileo" love that is a tender affection that friends or brothers and sisters have for one another. Scriptures emphasize our need for "koinonia" or fellowship, communion, sharing, and communication with one another (1 Corinthians 10:16, Philemon 6-7). Such sharing between Christians is essential to avoid burnout.

DO I NEED TO SET LIMITS?

Some people that we serve may be so needy that they try to consume every available moment of our time. They are so demanding that they can drain our energy and quickly make us question God's calling on our lives. These persons have difficulty setting boundaries between themselves and other people. They need others to set the boundaries for them. As we love and minister to the needs of these people, we must learn to set limits. If we cannot do this and give into other's expectations, then we become an *enabler*. In other words, we enable the person to continue acting in a neurotic or destructive way without giving him or her the feedback necessary for change. The following are two examples.

Sally forgives her alcoholic husband Bill over and over again for getting drunk and beating her. She even buys wine and beer for him because he asks her to. Sally is acting as an enabler. She is enabling her husband Bill to continue to act in a self-destructive and antisocial manner. The best thing for Bill would be if Sally set limits on what she will tolerate. In other words, if he gets drunk again, she should tell him that she will leave him (and then do it when he gets drunk). If he beats her again, she should tell him that she will call the police (and then call the police if he does beat her). Such limits will force Bill to get his act together, or suffer the consequences. The latest research shows that the primary reason why alcoholics stop drinking is because of the *negative consequences of their actions.*[2]

Tony is a disabled older man who wants Jim, a member of his church, to bring meals to him every night and spend hours listening to his problems. Tony does not wish to make any effort to help himself or use his own talents and abilities to get his needs met. He would rather manipulate and con other people like Jim to do these things for him. As a servant of Christ, should Jim love Tony by working hard to meet his every desire and wish? No. In this case, loving Tony means setting limits on his behavior. In other words, even though Tony cries and begs for Jim to come over to his house every night, Jim tells Tony that he will bring a meal over three times a week and will stay for one hour each time. When he comes over, Jim works with Tony to help him discover his own abilities and talents and how to use them. In other words, Jim helps Tony to become more self-sufficient and less dependent on him and other persons. This is real love–to want the very best for the other person. For some, this involves helping them to change even when they do not want to change. If we are unable to set limits as in the examples above, then we will allow the neurotic selfishness of others to consume not only their own lives, but ours as well.

DO I NEED TO PERSEVERE?

When ministering to others, at times it will seem as if very little progress is being made. This is particularly true in the area of counseling. Most of us want to see people get better. Sometimes, however, it just takes patience and perseverance. The people we serve, particularly those with unhealthy personality traits, are the way they are because of years and years of thinking and behaving in a certain way. It should not be surprising, then, that it may take years and years to see healthy changes take place in their lives. It is difficult, however, to project an attitude of hopefulness and encouragement to those who are discouraged when there is no visible progress. This is especially true when we are actually suffering with people, helping them shoulder their burdens. We want them to snap out of it because we ourselves may be tiring of the load. Ministry, then, becomes a trial. What is the Christian response?

> . . . make every effort to add to your faith, goodness; and to goodness, knowledge; and to knowledge, self-control; and to self-control, *perseverance*; and to perseverance, godliness; and to godliness, brotherly kindness, and to brotherly kindness, love. For if you possess these qualities in increasing measure they will keep you from being ineffective and unproductive . . . (2 Peter 1:5-8)

> Consider it pure joy, my brothers, whenever you face trials of many kinds, because you know that the testing of your faith develops *perseverance*. Perseverance must finish its work so that you may be mature and complete, not lacking anything. (James 1:2-4)

Blessed is the man who *perseveres* under trial, because when he has stood the test, he will receive the crown of life that God has promised to those who love him. (James 1:12)

Yes, perseverance is absolutely essential as we strive to become more and more Christ-like. Imagine Michelangelo chipping at the block of marble that was to become his great sculpture of David. God is using trial and suffering to chip away at our image to make us more like Christ. We must believe that there *will be* changes in the lives of those to whom we minister, though we may never see those changes or see them only years down the road. This knowledge will keep you from burning out, keep your hope alive for the person you are serving—indeed, *your hope* may be the only hope the person has.

AVOIDING THE GUILT TRAP

Maybe you are not using your gift. Then you should probably feel a bit guilty. But not all guilt is the same. Guilt can be marvelously motivating for some. It can be paralyzing and defeating for others. Many persons have difficulty distinguishing healthy from unhealthy guilt.

Healthy guilt is the type that keeps us from hurting others and moves us forward in our walk with God, often encouraging and prodding us into constructive action. The unhealthy kind is self-punishing, degrading, discouraging, and makes us feel bad, worthless, incapable. It pins a person down and will not let them up. Unhealthy guilt says "You are not using your gift. That is just the way you are. You never do anything right. You are worthless. You will never change. You are a failure." Healthy guilt, on the other hand, says "You have got a great talent, but you are not using it. Stop wasting your time. Let's get going. You can do it." If you feel a gentle, persistent tug at your heart, then that is probably healthy guilt. Remember that healthy guilt is energizing, not fatiguing, or demoralizing.

SUMMARY

This is one of the most important chapters in the book. We can easily become frustrated, discouraged, and hopeless when using our gifts to serve others, if we do not bear in mind certain precautions. First, we must remember why we are serving; we serve out of love for God. Second, we must remember who we are serving; we are serving God. Third, we must take time to rest–time to enjoy God's blessings, seek God's guidance, and refresh ourselves; we are commanded to do this because God knows that we will not last long if we are compulsively serving others without taking proper care of ourselves. Fourth, we must learn to share our experiences with other Christian brothers and sisters, seeking support and encouragement from each other. Fifth, we must learn to set limits on what we will do for persons who are excessively needy and overly-dependent; this not only for our good, but for their good as well. Sixth, we need to persevere when things are not proceeding as planned or expected; sometimes results are not forthcoming until many years down the road. At all times, extremes must be avoided and balance sought.

DISCUSSION QUESTIONS

1. Are you able to assess your motives objectively in your service to others? Have you asked yourself, "Why am I doing this?" "For whom am I doing this?"
2. If your focus is on serving the Lord Jesus Christ, and not focused on your fellow man, what can you expect the psychological and spiritual benefits to be?
3. What are some of the excesses or hindrances in using your talents or gifts that could lead to burnout?
4. Have you experienced "burnout" in your serving others, and if so, are you able to determine the cause/s?
5. Did you find it helpful to answer the six questions that are related to your service to others? Which of the six do you need to consider to insure healthy service?
6. How do you love yourself, even as you are called to love God and your neighbor?
7. Have you learned to set limits to your service to others? Would you share how and why you found this necessary?
8. If you are feeling guilty about not using your gifts, is this healthy or unhealthy guilt that you are experiencing? Have you asked God in prayer to show how your gifts may be used?

NOTES

1. "Burnout" is a condition characterized by exhaustion, fatigue, discouragement, or frustration that makes us want to quit loving and serving. The absence of joy and fulfillment is a signal of impending burnout. While we all feel like this at some time or another, it does not usually persist beyond a couple days. Such feelings must be dealt with as soon as they are recognized.

2. George Vaillant. Alcoholism taking the long view: 50-year review questions old assumptions. Information presented at the 1993 annual California Society of Addiction Medicine, November 1993. Commentary published in *Psychiatric Times* by Pamela Dilday-Davis, November 1994, pp. 6-7.

Chapter 12

Serving in Action

The purpose of this book has been to give you a vision. A vision that *you* can make a difference in this world now and for generations to come. This does not depend on your physical health, educational level, financial status, or living situation. God has given you a special talent for *this time* in your life so that you may use it to bring about God's kingdom on earth. We believe that these years of life, regardless of your circumstances, can be your best yet. Are you willing to commit yourself to the two great commandments of loving God and loving thy neighbor? If we in our "mature" years cannot, then when will we do it? And if we cannot, who can? Both our mental and spiritual growth depend on it, as does the welfare of our children and grandchildren in the generations to come. It is so simple, yet so difficult. So difficult, yet easier than carrying the burden the world would place on us–because serving God by serving others is ultimately one of the most effective ways of meeting our deepest psychological and spiritual needs.

Still, you may question whether all this is possible, whether it is actually do-able. Is it realistic for us to expect people to put aside their own needs and wants, and instead, use their talents to serve others in their community? Believe it or not, it does happen. We think it is appropriate to conclude this book with a real case that illustrates how Christians can use their special gifts to serve God by caring for and ministering to the needs of a neighbor touched by tragedy. We also describe a program that puts such principles to use on a community-wide basis.

LOVE THY NEIGHBOR

At the age of fifty-nine, Frank Kozoman[1] had his life pretty much together. He ran his own business (which was doing well), enjoyed his work, had a loving wife and supportive family, and lived in a beautiful two-level home. He was also actively involved in his local Christian church, a congregation of about 100 members. Frank was an intensely independent man. Years before he had quit his job so that he could call his own shots and not have to work under the direction of others. Since his coronary artery bypass surgery six years earlier, he had made quite an effort to keep himself in good physical shape and worked out several times per week at a local health club.

On December 16, 1995, Frank decided to put up some Christmas decorations on the eaves of his house. The North Carolina sky was clear, the sun was shining brightly, and the temperature was a warm 65 degrees. A perfect day to do a little work outside. He carefully set up a ladder that reached to the roof of the second story and climbed up with decorations in hand. When he got to the top, he began hanging the decorations. Frank spied his neighbor working in the yard next to him and yelled a greeting to him. "Life was good," he thought. After securing the last string of Christmas lights, Frank started down the ladder. Suddenly, the ladder spun and Frank's right leg got hung up in its rungs. He found himself falling backward heading for the ground some twenty-five to thirty feet below. Downward he fell, his head leading his body. Instinctively, Frank lifted his head upwards in a kind of mid-air situp. The full force of his body hit the hard ground with the point of impact being his mid-back region. He heard a sickening crunch. He bounced and rolled, winding up on his right side. Hearing the commotion, Frank's wife Susan rushed outside. At the same time, his neighbor ran over, lifted the ladder off him, and asked Frank if he could move his legs. He could not. Susan went back inside and called 911. The neighbor, a devout Christian, laid his hands gently on Frank's legs and began to pray for him.

The next few weeks were difficult ones for Frank and his wife. X rays revealed that Frank had broken four ribs, his right scapula, and right shoulder bone. Most ominously, the X rays showed that he had crushed his T-9 vertebrae (mid-back) which had splintered into his spinal cord. Surgery was performed to stabilize his spine, but the doctors could do nothing to return function to his legs. Frank had no sensation below his umbilicus. He had little control over his bowels or bladder. He could not move his legs at all. What he could feel, however, was excruciating pain in his middle back, rib cage, and right shoulder. The pain was continuous and exhausting. Powerful narcotic painkillers barely touched it. Rehabilitation was slow and difficult. He was completely dependent on the nursing staff. Frank had to be turned every couple hours to prevent bed sores. He had to learn how to catheterize himself every few hours to empty his bladder. Frank's life had changed. No longer was he the independent, self-sufficient businessman, husband, father, church and community leader of a couple weeks ago. Adjusting to this was hard for Frank and his wife. But they had some help.

Members of Frank's church visited him in the hospital. They brought him food. They listened. They prayed for him. They took his wife out to lunch and invited her over for dinner, and they listened. Bob, a retired IBM employee and computer expert, offered to help run Frank's business while he was in the hospital (without charge). Sam, a retired psychology professor, visited Frank every day in the hospital (without charge). He was gentle and kind, sometimes spending hours with Frank as he struggled to make sense of what had happened to him. While in the hospital, Frank longed for the time when he could return home. Other members of Frank's church helped as well. Bill, a contractor, and Tom, a painter, took time off from their jobs to make the alterations in Frank's home that were necessary before he could return there. They built a special bathroom that would make it easier for Frank to bathe himself and perform other self-care activities. No one charged Frank anything for the time. In fact, Richard, an elder in his church, asked Frank how he was doing financially, offering to help in that area if he needed it.

After two months in the hospital, Frank finally got the chance he had been waiting for. His doctors said he could go home. When Frank got home, however, things were different from what he had expected. The first two weeks were especially rough. Suicide frequently crossed his mind. Sam, his psychologist friend from church, continued to visit Frank at home, as did many other church members. They continued to bring meals, prayers, and fellowship—for both Frank and his wife. Every Sunday, the church as a group took time out in their service to pray for Frank and his family. Bob continued to help Frank with his business, volunteering several days each week for this purpose.

Slowly, but surely, Frank is getting his life back together. While his legs remain paralyzed, and he continues to suffer from severe chronic back pain, he has made use of the gifts that he has left–his two hands and arms and a quick mind. Frank is back running his business (with help from Bob) and supporting his family, working on the computer and on the telephone. His attitude is a realistic one, but full of hope and vision. When asked how he is getting through this difficult period in his life, his response was clear and certain. "My faith, my family, and my church," said Frank. He reached over and picked up his Bible, turned to Hebrews 11, verses 1-6, and began reading, "Now faith is being sure of what we hope for and certain of what we do not see . . . And without faith it is impossible to please God, because anyone who comes to him must believe that he exists and that he rewards those who earnestly seek him." This is what helped him get through. This and the love of other Christians in his life.

Frank's personal story shows what can happen when members of a church go out of their way to provide support and comfort to one of their own in need. It shows how both retired and actively working Christians can mobilize their current or previous talents to serve God in a practical way–by serving a neighbor in need. These people's actions affected and continue to affect not only Frank and his family, but also their own families–their children and grandchildren–who are watching how others behave around them. They are now exposed to role models of people helping people, people loving God "[not with mere] words or tongue but with actions and in truth" (1 John 3:18). These actions, then, create a ripple-effect that impacts the world not only now, but for generations to come.

A SERVING COMMUNITY

Not only did Frank's church rally to support him, but several times during the course of his illness, members of the broader Christian community–neighbors, nurses, aides, technicians, and even doctors–offered to lay hands on him and pray for him (which he accepted readily). This occurred at critical times in the course of

Frank's illness, when his physical or emotional pain were almost un-
bearable and no family members or members from his church were
around. Such spiritual encouragement brought him comfort and a
sense that he was not alone, that Someone greater was on his side,
working even through the health care providers around him. This
brings us to a larger question. How can *communities* organize themselves in a way that allows and encourages middle-aged and older
adults to mobilize their gifts and talents to serve God by serving each
other?

In the early 1980s, the Reverend Dr. Elbert Cole started what he
called a "Shepherds Center" in Kansas City, Missouri. This was a
community organization formed through the cooperation of local
churches and synagogues and supported by local businesses. It was
largely run and operated by persons over age fifty who volunteered
their time and talents to serve their peers in the community who
needed help in one form or another. Dr. Cole hired staff (many of
whom were over fifty) to work with, stimulate, encourage, and
support the development of hidden talents and expertise of those
participating in the center. Staff members were instructed to see
themselves as catalysts and deal with participants as partners who
themselves would maintain control and assume responsibility for
the program. This center, while initiated with a small government
grant, has for over ten years been maintained without government
funding. Local churches and businesses in the community donate
money to support the programs (which take place in vacated or
unused church space). The cost-effectiveness of this program has
become evident. It has served the needs of literally thousands of
homebound and disabled persons in the Kansas City area, enabling
many to continue living in their homes instead of having to move
into institutional settings.

With a volunteer staff of almost 400 aging adults, the Kansas City
Shepherd's Center now serves about 6,000 persons of all faiths living
in the community. Since its development in the early 1980s, over
eighty other centers have been established throughout the United
States, with over 100,000 older adults participating and over 15,000
home-bound elders receiving services. While a large number of persons participate in Shepherd's Center programs simply for the social

benefits (similar to a bridge club, rotary club, or senior center), many also participate in order to use their gifts to serve those in need. This program demonstrates the powerful effect that committed Christians can have on their surrounding community when they use their special God-given gifts and work together. We believe that it is possible to have a society where people of all ages, regardless of physical health, functional capacity, financial state, or social circumstances, serve one another, respect one another, lead meaningful and useful lives secure and filled with hope, joy, and purpose. It is possible only because of God; possible because it is part of God's plan and purpose as outlined in scripture; possible because human beings are closely connected with and affected by each other in a complex web of causation designed by our Creator. Is the vision of a world of committed Christians using their gifts to help one another not a vision worth working for and giving our lives to? Worth passing down to our children and grandchildren and great grandchildren?

SUMMARY

In this chapter we describe how a Christian community rallied to support one of their members in need. This case exemplifies how both actively working and retired persons can mobilize their talents to serve God by serving a neighbor. It also shows how someone with severe disability can, with God's help, cope with tragedy and mobilize their special gifts and talents to put their life back together. We also describe a community-wide program developed by and for older adults that puts many of the principles we've been discussing into practice.

DISCUSSION QUESTIONS

1. Reading about Shepherd's Centers above, would you like to see such a Center established in your community? Do see the possibility of your congregation becoming involved in such a project? Is your congregation now involved in any such program or project?

2. Can you see yourself personally responding to such a vision?
3. For the evaluation and future use of this group method, as a member of this group, will you share your reaction to this experience, both positive and negative? It would be helpful if this is recorded by you on paper.

NOTE

1. Frank has given us permission to use his real name; the names of other persons mentioned here are fictitious to protect their identity.

Final Prayer

Almighty and eternal God, whose presence surrounds us, and whose love is ever within our lives, so draw our hearts to you, so guide our minds, so fill our imaginations, so control our wills, that we may be wholly yours, dedicated to the gift of your love in our lives and in our neighbors'. Use us to your glory and to the welfare of your people in this world. We pray in the gift of the Holy Spirit, through your Son, Jesus Christ, our Lord. Amen.

Index

Ability. *See* Gifts; Talents
Abraham and Isaac, 57-58
Accounting as gift, 81
Action. *See also* Service
   importance of, 66-67
Adaptation to dependency,
   38-39,104-105
Adversity, 56-57. *See also* Suffering
   spiritual growth and, 24-25
Age
   at conversion, 25
   expected life span, 29-30
   spiritual growth and, 25
Aging
   definition of successful, 11-12
   in Western culture, 32
Alcoholism, 127
Allen, Charles, 78
Anger, 40,108
Appreciation, 79
Approval, service as seeking God's,
   121-122
Ark of the Covenant, 58
Artistic skill as gift, 81
Attitude
   negative, 40,85
   positive, 40,84-85

Balance, 8,119-129
Beauty of creation, 55-56
Being as opposed to performing,
   65-66
Bereavement, 38,46,115-116
Bible
   definition of, 13-14
   descriptions of God in, 50-53

Bible *(continued)*
   need to read and be inspired
      by, 43,113
   references to retirement absent
      from, 33
   as source of continuity, 109
Book of 1 John, 66
Book of the Law, 70
Brother Lawrence, 59-61,62,
   121-122
Burnout, 8,119-129
Business skills as gift, 81

Caretaking, respite, 80
Change
   economic, 30
   in gifts or talents, 87-89
   in health, 29-30
   implications for Church, 31
   necessity for, 20
   retirement and, 31-33
Character building, 61-62
Christ. *See* God; Jesus Christ
Christian, definition of, 13
Christian Church, implications
   of change for, 31
Christian Community, 136-138
   relationship with, 6-7,22
   social mission of, 31
Christian life, characteristics
   of, 23
Cleaning as gift, 80
Clergy as examples of godliness, 53
Closer Than a Brother (Winter),
   59-61,62
Cole, Dr. Elbert, 137-138

Order Your Own Copy of
This Important Book for Your Personal Library!

A GOSPEL FOR THE MATURE YEARS
Finding Fulfillment by Knowing and Using Your Gifts

_____ in hardbound at $39.95 (ISBN: 0-7890-0158-6)

_____ in softbound at $19.95 (ISBN: 0-7890-0170-5)

COST OF BOOKS_____

OUTSIDE USA/CANADA/
MEXICO: ADD 20%_____

POSTAGE & HANDLING_____
(US: $3.00 for first book & $1.25
for each additional book)
Outside US: $4.75 for first book
& $1.75 for each additional book)

SUBTOTAL_____

IN CANADA: ADD 7% GST_____

STATE TAX_____
(NY, OH & MN residents, please
add appropriate local sales tax)

FINAL TOTAL_____
(If paying in Canadian funds,
convert using the current
exchange rate. UNESCO
coupons welcome.)

☐ **BILL ME LATER:** ($5 service charge will be added)
(Bill-me option is good on US/Canada/Mexico orders only;
not good to jobbers, wholesalers, or subscription agencies.)

☐ Check here if billing address is different from
shipping address and attach purchase order and
billing address information.

Signature_____

☐ **PAYMENT ENCLOSED: $**_____

☐ **PLEASE CHARGE TO MY CREDIT CARD.**

☐ Visa   ☐ MasterCard   ☐ AmEx   ☐ Discover

Account # _____

Exp. Date _____

Signature _____

Prices in US dollars and subject to change without notice.

NAME _____

INSTITUTION _____

ADDRESS _____

CITY _____

STATE/ZIP _____

COUNTRY _____ COUNTY (NY residents only) _____

TEL _____ FAX _____

E-MAIL_____
May we use your e-mail address for confirmations and other types of information? ☐ Yes   ☐ No

Order From Your Local Bookstore or Directly From
The Haworth Press, Inc.
10 Alice Street, Binghamton, New York 13904-1580 • USA
TELEPHONE: 1-800-HAWORTH (1-800-429-6784) / Outside US/Canada: (607) 722-5857
FAX: 1-800-895-0582 / Outside US/Canada: (607) 772-6362
E-mail: getinfo@haworth.com
PLEASE PHOTOCOPY THIS FORM FOR YOUR PERSONAL USE.

BOF96